Quik Notes
Christian
Classics

Quiknotes™

CHRISTIAN
CLASSICS

General Editor:
Philip W. Comfort, Ph.D.
Department of Biblical and Theological Studies
Wheaton College

with

Daniel Partner

Edited by David P. Barrett

Tyndale House Publishers, Inc.
WHEATON, ILLINOIS

Visit Tyndale's exciting Web site at www.tyndale.com

Library of Congress Cataloging-in-Publication Data

Quik notes on Christian classics / general editor, Philip W. Comfort, with Daniel Partner ;
    editor, David P. Barrett.
      p. cm.
    Includes bibliographical references.
    ISBN 0-8423-5986-9 (pbk. : alk. paper)
    1. Spiritual life—Christianity.   2. Devotional exercises.   3. Devotional literature.
    I. Comfort, Philip Wesley. II. Partner, Daniel. III. Barrett, David P.
    IV. Title: Quick notes on Christian classics.
BV4501.2.Q55   1999
242—dc20   95-40488

Printed in the United States of America

04   03   02   01   00   99
7   6   5   4   3   2

Introduction

THROUGHOUT the history of the Christian church, certain books have become classics of the faith, inspiring and instructing countless readers. Some books have fundamentally changed the way Christians have understood their faith; others have simply inspired readers to become better Christians.

For various reasons, however, many Christians today are unfamiliar with these classic works of Christianity. The purpose of this collection of summaries is to give readers a beginning list of these books and to give a short synopsis of their content.

To compile such an abridged list of classics from the myriad of possible selections inevitably requires that certain books be left out, though many readers may consider them significant. In order to give some direction to the selection process, the editors of this collection established a few basic guidelines for selecting each book. In order for a work to be included, it should meet these criteria. (1) It has stood the test of time and continues to be recognized by Christians as a significant Christian work. (2) It has been widely read, significantly impacting many readers. (3) It accurately represents the author's overall beliefs and concerns that may appear in his or her other works as well.

In order to help the reader better understand the historical and biographical setting of the works, a brief outline of the life of each author is given along with a summary of his work. Often this background information helps explain many of the concerns and emphases that are evident in the works. The books have also been arranged chronologically to help the reader grasp the development of popular Christian history and thought.

The Early Church Fathers

Didache (Teaching)   c. 90

The *Didache*, or "The Teaching of the Lord to the Gentiles through the Twelve Apostles," is a manual of church discipline. Its origin and date are difficult to determine precisely, but scholars generally agree that it was written in Syria during the second half of the first century. The practices described in the manual were established much earlier, however. The *Didache* was compiled from various sources that detail the traditions of well-established church communities.

This handbook contains a number of texts that were intended to instruct new converts in the Christian faith. Chapters 1–6 present the "Two Ways" of life and death, based on Deuteronomy 30:15. This section resembles many Jewish teachings and may find its source in the apocalyptic writings of the Qumran community (where the Dead Sea Scrolls were compiled). The manual also contains several parallels with the *Epistle of Barnabas* and *The Shepherd* by Hermas. These first chapters include a distinctly Christian collection of sayings that resemble Jesus' teachings about loving one's neighbor (as recorded by Matthew and Luke).

Chapters 7–10 contain instructions for baptism, fasting,

prayer, and the Eucharist. Baptism is to be performed "in the name of the Father, Son, and Holy Spirit"; fasting is to be practiced on Wednesdays and Fridays, in contrast with the Jews who fasted on Mondays and Thursdays; and the Lord's Prayer (with the Doxology) is to be recited daily. The prayers in chapters 9 and 10 are based on Jewish table prayers, so it is not clear whether they are meant for the Eucharist or for a common church meal (sometimes called a "love feast"). The prayers contain no references to the words of Jesus at the Last Supper, and they place the blessing of the cup before the blessing of the bread (cf. 1 Corinthians 10:16). The *Didache* does note that believers are not required to use these model prayers.

Chapters 11–15 give instructions for church leadership. They discuss the marks of true apostles and prophets, who are referred to as "high priests," and the church's responsibilities toward them. The *Didache* ends with a prediction of the imminent return of Christ.

The Jewishness of the *Didache* may reflect the influence of the Jerusalem church's teachings. The description of church leadership, however, seems to be drawn from Paul, who details the roles of apostles, prophets, and teachers in 1 Corinthians. The *Didache* also stresses the function of the prophets. The teachings of the *Didache* reflect those of a church in the developmental stages of its institutions and practices. The church still appears to be developing characteristics that clearly distinguish it from Judaism. The *Didache* was highly regarded by the early church. Eusebius listed it with the orthodox writings that were eventually excluded from the New Testament canon.

Epistle of Clement   c. 96
Clement of Rome
. . . .

Clement was a bishop in Rome who wrote a letter to the church at Corinth around 96. This letter is probably the earliest extant

Christian epistle outside the New Testament. Around 170, Dionysius of Corinth recorded the earliest claim that Clement was the author of this letter. Origen and Eusebius also identified Clement as the epistle's author.

Clement's epistle to the Corinthians admonishes several younger believers who led a revolt and ousted the leading elders of the Corinthian church. These young men may have wanted a more flexible system of ministry and recognition of their spiritual gifts. They were ascetics and claimed a secret knowledge *(gnosis)* of the faith that was revealed only to the elite.

This letter was sent from the entire Roman church rather than from a single individual. The early churches did not consider themselves to be isolated loners. They knew they were a part of the universal church and were not immune to the events and conditions of their sister congregations. They felt responsible to warn and advise each other.

The Septuagint (the Greek translation of the Old Testament) is cited often in this letter. The heroes of the Old Testament are held up as patterns for Christian conduct, thereby mingling New Testament and Old Testament themes. The apostle Paul's first letter to the Corinthians is the pattern for Clement's letter to the same church. Clement closely imitates 1 Corinthians 13 in chapters 49 and 50, and he grounds many of his beliefs in Paul's writings regarding the resurrection and schisms. But Clement's writing is moralistic and ethical and often more akin to Hellenistic Judaism and Stoicism than to Pauline theology. Clement also describes a hierarchical form of ministry and endorses the doctrine of apostolic succession.

Clement quoted extensively from the words of Jesus, using sayings found in Matthew, Mark, and Luke. He also quoted Romans, 1 Corinthians, and Hebrews. Thus Clement provides important evidence that books that later became part of the New Testament canon were circulating among the churches by the end of the first century. Clement's letter also provides important evidence for the martyrdom of the apostles Peter and Paul and for Paul's mission to the "western boundary" (i.e., Spain?).

Epistle to the Romans   c. 116
Ignatius of Antioch
. . . .

Ignatius was bishop of Syrian Antioch and a martyr in Rome under the emperor Trajan (c. 116). He wrote seven letters while en route to Rome under armed guard. In his letter to the Romans, Ignatius disclosed, "I am [chained] to ten savage leopards [soldiers], who only grow more insolent the more gratuities they are given. Still, their ill-usage does at least enable me to make some progress in discipleship" (5:1-2). The letters were written to churches who maintained ties with him throughout his journey: Philadelphia, Smyrna, Ephesus, Tralles, and Magnesia. He sent a letter ahead to the church in Rome to prevent it from interceding with the authorities on his behalf. He also wrote a letter to Polycarp, the bishop of Smyrna.

Ignatius devoted much of his writing to combating various heresies that were creeping into the churches. He opposed the Ebionite heresy, which demanded the keeping of the Jewish regulations as the way of salvation. Ignatius insisted instead that believers must reject all Jewish practices in order to affirm Christ. Nevertheless, he understood the church to be the continuation of the Old Testament people of God. Ignatius likewise attacked Docetism, which held that Christ only *appeared* to have a real birth, death, and resurrection. Ignatius reaffirmed the physical facts of Christ's life, and he is the first writer outside the New Testament to speak of the virgin birth of Jesus. He also affirmed that the apostles touched the body of the risen Lord.

Ignatius also affirmed the importance of the bishop in church structure. Ignatius insisted that it is not permissible to conduct baptisms or the Lord's Supper without the bishop. This early emphasis on the bishop suggests that the church rapidly developed an episcopal structure of government. In the New Testament, the local church was governed by a body of officers called elders or bishops, but by the time of Ignatius, there are references to a single ruling bishop in each city except Rome. Ignatius is also the first writer to use the term *catholic* (universal) to describe the church.

In contrast to Ignatius's other six letters, the *Epistle to the Romans* contains no caution against heresy, no mention of the bishop, and no admonition to unity. Instead, through lyrical prose, Ignatius glories in his coming martyrdom, which he compares to an acceptable sacrifice to God. He appeals to the Romans not to interfere with the authorities and obtain his pardon. Ignatius asserts that the suffering and resurrection of Jesus Christ have made it possible for him to face martyrdom. In the following centuries, persecuted Christians were strongly influenced by this epistle, making it Ignatius's most popular work. It became the "martyr's manual" of Christendom.

Epistle to the Philippians   c. 120
Polycarp
. . . .

Born to a Christian family, Polycarp identified himself as a disciple of John, presumably the apostle. Polycarp was appointed bishop of Smyrna in Asia Minor. Ignatius of Antioch, on his way to Roman martyrdom (c. 116), wrote letters to Polycarp and to the church at Smyrna. Near the end of his life, Polycarp visited Rome. He was serving as representative of the Asia Minor churches in a discussion over the observance of Easter. Polycarp was later arrested by civil authorities, who attempted to convince him to renounce his faith. When he refused, he was burned at the stake. The story of Polycarp's death (recounted in a letter from the church of Smyrna to the church of Philomelium) is the earliest record of Christian martyrdom outside the New Testament.

As bishop of Smyrna, Polycarp wrote many letters to various churches. Only one of Polycarp's letters has survived, however. This letter, addressed to the Philippians, was written in response to a letter they had sent him. Apparently, while Ignatius was on his way to martyrdom in Rome, his guards chose to make a stop in Philippi. While there, Ignatius encouraged the local church to write to the church in Antioch. So they sent a letter by way of Polycarp of Smyrna. They also requested copies of Ignatius's letters to the Asian churches.

Polycarp's reply to Philippi is the document now called his *Epistle to the Philippians,* written around 120. It is the only example of the writing of this early church father. In his letter Polycarp assumes that Ignatius has already suffered death, but it seems that he is not certain of this. He asks the Philippians to send him what news they may have of Ignatius.

In his epistle, Polycarp mentions the fame of the Philippians among the churches from the early days to that time. He refers to the apostle Paul's instructions for the church there, making reference to more than one letter from the apostle. Polycarp warns against the love of money, which caused the downfall of one of the leaders of the church. He also warns against those who deny the resurrection of Christ, the Docetist heretics. Polycarp instructs the Philippians on the duties of church leaders and other Christians. It is often noted that, unlike Ignatius who stressed episcopacy, Polycarp does not mention the bishop.

While many critics have labeled Polycarp's letter "unoriginal," containing no new theological insights, the letter does provide insight into the available New Testament writings for the churches. There are no citations from the Old Testament in this epistle, but there are quotations and allusions to Matthew, Acts,

Romans, 1 Corinthians, Galatians, Ephesians, 2 Thessalonians, 1 Timothy, and 1 Peter. He also makes use of Clement's epistle and the Ignatian letters. It is interesting to note that Polycarp makes no reference to the Gospel of John, though tradition insists that he was a disciple of the apostle John.

The letter ends with Polycarp's promise to forward the Philippians' letter to Antioch. He also promises to send them Ignatius's letters.

Epistle of Barnabas   c. 130

This anonymous letter addresses a question commonly asked throughout the early church: What should Christianity's relationship be to Judaism? Clement of Alexandria quoted from this document frequently and ascribed it to "Barnabas, who himself also preached with the apostle [Paul]." Jerome believed the same. But the writer does not claim to be Barnabas, and the earliest claims of authorship come only from Alexandrian church leaders. The literary and interpretive style is entirely Alexandrian, so it is assumed that the epistle was written in Alexandria.

The author of this epistle unequivocally denies any connection between Judaism and the gospel of Jesus Christ. At the same time, he does not say that the Old Testament opposes the New Testament; rather, he sees Christianity everywhere in the Law and the Prophets. He holds that all the Judaistic rites and ceremonies are mystical pointers to Christ and that an evil angel has blinded the Jews from understanding this.

The epistle mentions the destruction of Jerusalem, so it was not written before 70. There was a second devastation of Jerusalem in 132 that ended the revolt of Bar-Cochba. This defeat would have served the author's purposes so well that he would surely have referred to it if he were writing after the event. Many scholars suggest that the letter was composed around 130, since this was a period of strong Jewish nationalism. This nationalism would have pressured many Jewish Christians to return to Judaism, and so the author of the *Epistle of Barnabas* wrote to defend Christianity against Judaism.

The *Epistle of Barnabas* is composed of two parts. The first section (chapters 1–17) contains allegorical interpretations of the Old Testament. These highly spiritual and mystical interpretations are intended to oppose Jewish legalism and explain how the Old Testament prophesied of Jesus Christ. The author concedes that righteous people, such as Moses, David, and the prophets, understood the true meaning of Mosaic law, but he contends that the rest of the nation of Israel had misconstrued God's covenant. Therefore, the Jews lost their claim to the covenant's blessings, which were transferred to the Christians instead. This allegorical style of interpretation was very popular among Alexandrian church leaders. The New Testament epistle of Hebrews also makes use of this type of interpretation. The author of the *Epistle of Barnabas* often quotes from the Septuagint, though the quotes are somewhat loosely recited.

A Latin version of the first section was all that was known of the *Epistle of Barnabas* until the discovery of the Codex Sinaiticus in 1859. This codex contained the first known Greek version of the *Epistle of Barnabas,* which was appended to the books of the New Testament along with *The Shepherd* and the *Didache.* The Greek version contains a second section that begins, "Now let us pass on to quite a different sort of instruction." This section contains moral precepts that contrast the way of darkness with the way of light, much of which seems to be transcribed from the "Two Ways" of the *Didache.* It has little connection with the first section. This has led many scholars to conclude that the second section was added by another writer at some later date.

The Shepherd   c. 150
Hermas
. . . .

Not much is known of Hermas other than the details he includes of himself in his work *The Shepherd.* In this story, Hermas states that he was originally a slave. He eventually gained his freedom, married, started a business, lost nearly everything, watched his children stray, and finally reunited his family. Hermas indicates that he knew Clement, the first-century bishop of Rome. From internal evidences, it is impossible to tell whether this biography is fictional or not. As to external facts, references to Hermas are contradictory. In the third century, Origen thought Hermas was the individual Paul mentions in Romans 16:14. Other authorities, including the second-century Muratorian Canon, identified Hermas as a brother of Pius, bishop of Rome around 150. Most scholars today favor this second position. Irenaeus, bishop of Lyons, provided the first recorded reference to *The Shepherd* in 185.

In *The Shepherd,* Hermas describes a series of visions about Christian life and morality. Throughout the story Hermas is both the hero and the narrator. The story is set in Rome and is divided into three parts: five visions, twelve mandates, and ten similitudes, or parables.

Five visions allegorize Christian ethical truths with such symbolism as a tower under construction and an older woman who becomes youthful. The visions begin with Hermas as he is smitten by the beautiful Rhoda to whom he is sold as a slave. In the second vision Rhoda reappears as an old woman, representing the church. This old woman becomes more youthful each time she appears. The visions portray the church growing and spreading, purified by suffering and, in the fourth vision, by the terrors of judgment.

It is in the fifth vision, while Hermas is in his own house, that he no longer sees the church, but a bright glowing man appears dressed like a shepherd. The man has been sent to live with Hermas to teach him until his death. The man is "the Shepherd, the angel of repentance" who gives Hermas twelve mandates and ten similitudes, which form the remaining sections of the work.

In brief, the twelve mandates depict Christian virtues—humility, chastity, truthfulness, long-suffering, simplicity, respectfulness, and good cheer. The mandates also exhort believers to purity and repentance. Prominent here is the "Two Ways" pattern of moral instruction (the way of life and the way of death). This mirrors the *Didache* and other early Christian ethical writings.

Finally, the ten similitudes describe principles by which the Christian virtues may be attained. The similitudes consider such topics as Christians as strangers, the rich and the poor, the sinners and the righteous, blossoming and withered trees, the purpose of the commandments, fasting, and punishment. They also include long parables about branches, a tower, maidens, and mountains. The tenth similitude is not a parable but a concluding chapter to summarize the work of the Shepherd. Here Hermas sums up the focus of the book: "I, too, sir, declare to every person the mighty works of the Lord; for I hope that all who have sinned in the past, if they hear these things, will gladly repent and recover life."

Throughout the early church, leaders gave Hermas's book high respect. Eusebius of Caesarea noted that *The Shepherd* was read widely in the early church. Some important leaders, such as Irenaeus and Clement of Alexandria, even considered it canonical Scripture. For Athanasius the work was not Scripture, but it did offer, like the *Didache,* help for Christian learners. Because of its simplicity and candor, some have compared Hermas's work with Bunyan's *The Pilgrim's Progress. The Shepherd* served as a valuable index to Christian ethics and moral instruction in Christianity's earliest decades.

Against Heresies c. 185
Irenaeus
. . . .

Irenaeus grew up in Asia Minor under the preaching of Polycarp, bishop of Smyrna. He later moved to southern France, becoming an elder in Lyons. After the aging bishop there was martyred, Irenaeus succeeded him as bishop in the West.

Much of Irenaeus's energies were spent combating various heresies that were infiltrating the church. In his primary work, *Against Heresies,* Irenaeus presents his theology as statements of the Christian faith in order to refute the heresies of Valentinus (the Gnostic) and Marcion. For Irenaeus the authority of the Christian faith is established through the direct line of bishops in the church, reaching back to the apostles themselves. The authentic message preserved through the church confirms the Christian Bible. Irenaeus also produced a list of books that were considered "Scripture" along with the Old Testament.

Irenaeus's writings were more Pauline than the apostolic fathers' works. His arguments were also grounded more in Scripture than in philosophy, unlike many other Greek church leaders who came after him. Although he was a contemporary of Christian apologists, Irenaeus was the first to write as a theologian for the church.

Irenaeus's composition *Against Heresies* was written at the request of a friend and is usually dated around 185. Its oldest manuscripts exist only in a Latin version from the early third century. A major part of the first book has been preserved in the original Greek, however, because it is thoroughly quoted in the writings of Hippolytus, Epiphanius, and others.

Against Heresies is devoted to describing and refuting Gnosticism, a philosophical movement that was spreading throughout the early church. Eventually Gnosticism was defeated by Irenaeus, Clement of Alexandria, and others, and its writings were almost entirely destroyed. As a result, before 1940, scholars of Gnosticism were largely dependent on the writings of Irenaeus, who carefully summarized the Gnostic teachings before refuting them. When a Gnostic library near Nag Hammadi was discovered in the 1940s, its contents revealed that Irenaeus had been very precise in his description of various heresies.

Against Heresies is divided into five books: Book 1 gives minute descriptions of different heretical sects and counters each with an argument from reason or Scripture. Book 2 discusses the traits of false *gnosis* and traces the history of Gnosticism, arguing against it on the basis of reason. In book 3 Irenaeus contends that true teaching is based on Scripture, and book 4 continues this same theme. Book 4 establishes that the God of the Old Testament is the same God who is revealed in Jesus of Nazareth in the New Testament. Book 5 addresses definite future events, such as the resurrection of believers, in order to contrast Christianity with the spiritualized beliefs of Gnosticism. Here Irenaeus adopts the view of the future described in the Revelation of John.

As Irenaeus combated Gnostic beliefs in *Against Heresies,* he also laid the groundwork for establishing the New Testament canon. The second century was a hotbed for works claiming scriptural authority, and some of these were written by Gnostics. By his attacks on Gnosticism, Irenaeus helped diminish the value of Gnostic works, which were eventually removed from the list of authoritative works.

Irenaeus is also famous for his "recapitulation theory" of redemption. This theory asserts that Jesus traversed the same ground as Adam, but he did so to reverse the curse of sin. Jesus experienced every phase of human development and sanctified them by his obedience. It was through his obedience that sin and death were defeated.

Nicene Creed   325/381
. . . .

The first ecumenical council of the Christian church was called
by the emperor Constantine in 325 and was held at Nicea in Asia
Minor. About three hundred bishops gathered for the proceedings. All but six of them were from the Eastern Empire. The
chief purpose of this council was to deal with controversy in the
church, notably that which had been stirred up by the Alexandrian theologian Arius. His teaching, known as Arianism, began
with the concept of God as absolute. It followed that everything
else was created by the one God, including the Son of God.
Arius held that there could not be a plurality of persons in one
God and that if the Son was created, he could not be of the same
nature as the Father. Christ was not the essential Son of God,
declared Arius, but only the adopted one. Such views led to
Arius's excommunication by the bishop of Alexandria, but this
merely increased the number of Arius's supporters.

The largest party at Nicea was led by Eusebius of Caesarea.
This party wanted to adopt a creed that accepted the divinity of
Christ while still allowing room for Arian claims. Eusebius's
creed was rejected.

Finally, a deacon from Alexandria named Athanasius champi-
oned what has since become orthodox belief regarding the person of Jesus Christ. Like his adversary Arius, Athanasius was not
a member of the council but could speak by invitation.
Athanasius contended successfully for the orthodox doctrine of
God and creation against Arius's arguments. Athanasius saw the
whole issue in terms of great principles, not of theological subtle-
ties. Largely through Athanasius's intervention, the council
squarely countered Arian assertions by insisting on three points:
(1) the Son was *out of the being of the Father*; (2) the Son was
begotten, not made; (3) the Son was of *the same nature with the*

Father rather than merely of *a similar nature to that of the Father.*

A creed was drawn up to include these assertions and to denounce those who affirmed Arian beliefs. This creed was probably modified from a Jerusalem baptismal creed. It was ratified by a majority of the bishops present. Another council was held at Constantinople in 381, and a second creed was produced, modifying and expanding the original one. Its text is as follows:

We believe in one God, the Father, the Almighty, maker of heaven and earth, of all that is visible and invisible.

We believe in one Lord, Jesus Christ, the only Son of God, eternally begotten of the Father, God from God, Light from Light, true God from true God, begotten, not made, of one Being with the Father; through him all things were made. For us and for our salvation he came down from heaven: By the power of the Holy Spirit he was born of the Virgin Mary and became human. For our sake he was crucified under Pontius Pilate; he suffered death and was buried. On the third day he rose again, in accordance with the Scriptures; he ascended into heaven and is seated at the right hand of the Father. He will come again in glory to judge the living and the dead, and his kingdom will have no end.

We believe in the Holy Spirit, the Lord, the giver of life, who proceeds from the Father, who with the Father and the Son is worshiped and glorified, who has spoken through the prophets. We believe in the one holy, catholic, and apostolic church. We acknowledge one baptism for the forgiveness of sins. We look for the resurrection of the dead and the life of the world to come. Amen.

Two dissident bishops were deposed when the Nicene Creed was adopted and, along with Arius and his colleagues, were condemned and banished. After the Council of Nicaea, disobedience to church decisions was regarded as a crime against the state.

Although Athanasius made powerful enemies at Nicea, he became bishop of Alexandria three years after the council.

Vulgate c. 400
Jerome
. . . .

Born into wealth near Aquileia (northern Italy), Jerome spent his youth acquiring a broad education in Rome. No descriptions of his conversion remain, but at about age twenty he was baptized. Soon thereafter Jerome embarked on a twenty-year period of travel, a pilgrimage traversing the empire. This pilgrimage began at Trier (France), where Jerome studied theology for several years and acquired a lifelong attraction to monasticism. Returning to Aquileia, he remained three years with Bishop Valerianus and an ascetic sect. But in 375, very discontented, Jerome moved to Antioch, Syria. Here he experienced a conscience-stricken dream in which he was accused of following Cicero rather than Christ. Jerome later recalled that his commitment to Christianity underwent a significant transformation because of this incident.

Shortly after the dream, Jerome withdrew to the desert around Chalcis (east of Antioch). Here he began an intense study of Scripture and embarked on a search to understand himself in relation to his Christianity. Upon his return to Antioch two years later, Jerome was ordained as a priest by Bishop Paulinus. Here he was influenced by the teaching of Apollinaris of Laodicea. Moving to Constantinople, he spent two years as a disciple of Gregory of Nazianzus, the great teacher whose circle included Basil of Caesarea, Gregory of Nyssa, and other eminent church figures. During this period, Jerome was heavily influenced by the writings of Origen. Jerome's wandering concluded in the years 382 to 385, the happiest and most fruitful segment of his pilgrimage.

Jerome returned to Rome to serve as Pope Damasus's personal

secretary. There he pursued his chief interests: the study of Scripture and the practice of monastic asceticism. This period ended abruptly, however, due to Damasus's death and conflicts stirred up by Jerome's often sour personality. In much disarray, Jerome left Rome to seek a place for the remote, unfettered monastic life he found so important. He finally settled in Bethlehem, Palestine, in 386. Here he spent his last thirty-five years deeply engaged in biblical scholarship and translation.

Jerome's many works may be grouped under six headings: translation of the Bible, commentaries on Scripture, translation of others' works, historical treatises, theological essays, and letters and miscellaneous works. It appears that none of Jerome's works have been lost over the centuries. There are even a few medieval copies of his Bible translation still in existence.

The term *Vulgate* comes from the Latin *edito vulgata,* which means "common version." The Vulgate was the Latin Bible used by the Roman Catholic Church from the early Middle Ages until the Second Vatican Council (1962). Jerome was the primary translator of this version, which he began while secretary to Pope Damasus I. The pope had suggested in 382 that the Old Latin version that was being used at the time needed correction.

Jerome first revised the Gospels. These appeared in 383. He also completed the Psalms before Damasus died and Jerome lost his patronage. Then from a monastery in Bethlehem, Jerome continued his translation work, though often against strong opposition. In the *Hexapla* of Origen, Jerome had access to the Septuagint, the Greek translation of the Old Testament. From that he translated into Latin the books of Job, 1 and 2 Chronicles, Proverbs, Ecclesiastes, and the Song of Songs. He also translated the Psalms again. This version of the Psalms came to be known as the *Gallican Psalter,* an important part of Roman Catholic liturgy and breviary. Later Jerome quit using the Greek Old Testament and began translating from the original Hebrew texts around 389; he completed his Latin version of the Old Testament in 405.

Jerome did nearly all of his work by private initiative, so his translation was slow to be accepted by the church. The Old Latin version was extremely familiar and was not easily abandoned. In addition, the Greek church leaders held the Septuagint to be divinely inspired, so some leaders thought that the Vulgate would sever ties between the Latin and the Greek churches. There was even a riot in Tripoli when the Vulgate version of Jonah was brought into the church.

Jerome was stubborn, however, and held out against all his critics. In time the Vulgate was vindicated, and by the middle of the sixth century, a complete Bible within a single cover was in use. This contained Jerome's Old Testament, his *Gallican Psalter,* his translations of Tobit and Judith, and his revision of the Gospels. Older Latin versions completed his New Testament. These may also have been revised by Jerome. Older versions of the Apocrypha were also included. In 1546 the Council of Trent designated the Vulgate as the exclusive Latin authority for the Bible.

The Middle Ages

Confessions and *City of God*   c. 410
Augustine of Hippo
. . . .

Augustine was born in the North African town of Tagaste. He
was the son of a pagan father, Patricius, and a Christian mother,
Monica. With great personal sacrifice, both parents sought the
best Roman education for their gifted son as a key to his
advancement from their small town. Augustine studied first at
Madauros and then received training in rhetoric at Carthage
(375). There Augustine abandoned the faith of his mother,
joining in the immoral practices of his fellow students. In 372 he
took a mistress, who remained with him for about thirteen years
and bore him a son, Adeodatus.

While reading Cicero's *Hortensius* (now lost), Augustine was
stirred to a religious quest for wisdom through philosophy. His
quest took him to the Manichaean sect, where he remained for
nine years. The Manichaeans understood the world as a grand
interplay between two equally powerful forces, one being an absolute evil power and the other an absolute good power. According
to this sect, the God of the Old Testament was the evil being, and
the God of Christianity was the good one. Augustine adopted these

views of the Old Testament and of personal evil, excusing his own conduct by blaming his actions on the evil nature within him. Eventually, however, he abandoned the Manichaeans when their expert, Faustus, was unable to resolve some basic problems Augustine had with their views. The disappointed teacher of rhetoric moved to Rome to start his own school.

During Augustine's brief stay in Rome, he turned to the writings of the Skeptics (Academics), who said that true knowledge was not obtainable. These thoughts, along with financial problems caused by delinquent students, caused Augustine to despair. Through a contact with a senator, Symmachus, Augustine was appointed professor of rhetoric in Milan (384). He was later appointed to the residence of the Roman emperor himself. As part of his appointment, Augustine was to give the public oration honoring the emperor Valentinian II.

While in Rome, Augustine attended the preaching of the Christian bishop Ambrose in order to hear his eloquence, and Ambrose's allegorical preaching began to answer many of the questions Augustine had raised with the Manichaeans. Although Augustine could not bring himself to converse with the busy Ambrose, he sought out Christian intellectuals in Milan, who instructed him and gave him Latin translations of the Neoplatonist writers Plotinus and Porphyry. While these writers failed to clearly point Augustine to Christ, they did engender in him a spiritual struggle over morality. In time Augustine read the New Testament book of Romans and came to understand Christ as a moral authority over him, giving him a "new will." After a sudden moral conversion, Augustine abandoned his teaching position and withdrew with some close friends and relatives to a friend's villa at Cassiciacum in order to pursue truth.

With confidence that a purified soul was able to arrive at clear truth, Augustine engaged the group at Cassiciacum in Socratic dialogue, a method in which a teacher directs questions to individuals in a group and leads them in the discussion, yet often without conclusion. The dialogues, recorded by a scribe and later supplemented by Augustine, were the basis of three of his writings. He later said of these early works that he had too high a regard for the teachings of the Platonists at the time and was still influenced by their school of pride. Augustine received baptism from Ambrose on Easter of 387, and in 388 he returned to North Africa after the death of his mother.

For a two-year period at Tagaste, Augustine supervised and instructed a group of baptized laymen. The North African church was then struggling against the influence of the Manichaeans and the Donatists. Many congregations were without the guidance of a bishop. On a visit to Hippo, Augustine was compelled by the congregation to become their priest. The bishop there spoke Latin with difficulty, unlike Augustine. After further study of the Bible, Augustine served as priest, and in 396 he became bishop of Hippo, where he would remain until his death.

On August 28, 410, troops of the barbarian king Alaric entered and sacked Rome, sending shock waves throughout the empire that shook both pagans and Christians. The pagans blamed the fall of the city on the Christians, who had deserted the old gods. The Christians had no reply because they had claimed that God would protect the empire of the Christian emperors. Refugees reaching North Africa demanded an answer from Augustine. His answer to them came through his work *City of God*.

Among the refugees who came to Africa from Rome were some who stirred a controversy in the Roman church over God's grace and human freedom. The leading figure was Pelagius, an ascetic layman from Britain who drew followers in Rome to his monastic ideal. Pelagius taught that human nature was capable of perfection and that the demands of God could be carried out completely, since no one is born with original sin. Pelagius was an activist who wanted to reform society through the young noblemen converted to his ideal. He also criticized Augustine's dependence upon grace, insisting that it was merely an encouragement to laziness. Pelagius moved from Africa to Jerusalem without ever meeting Augustine; but Pelagius's outspoken pupil, Celestius, remained in Africa to apply for the office of priest. Through the efforts of Augustine, the Council of Carthage (411) condemned Celestius as a heretic for his Pelagian views. From 412 until the end of his life, Augustine wrote thirteen works and letters against the Pelagians.

During the last months of Augustine's life, the Vandals held the fortified town of Hippo under siege by land and sea. They had destroyed Roman North Africa and much of Latin Christianity. Hippo was filled with refugees, including bishops and priests. Augustine preached to a congregation filled with refugees and had the golden vessels of the church melted down to give aid to the many who came. Augustine's letters acknowledged that Africa was ripe for God's judgment at the hands of the barbarians. During this crisis, the seventy-five-year-old Augustine contracted a fatal disease and eventually died.

The measure of Augustine's importance goes beyond the rare title "Doctor of the Church," given to him later in the Middle Ages. His introspective autobiography, *Confessions,* gave the church a clear picture of a life undergoing the transformation of the Christian gospel. *City of God* gave the church a systematic, biblical view of history and the state. He established much doctrine for the church in his anti-Donatist writings, and he gave the Western church a clear statement concerning the person of Christ. Augustine made the grace of God the theme of theology in the West.

As a mature theologian, Augustine wrote *Confessions,* the best known of his writings. This emotionally moving book is an autobiography, a testimony, in a sense, of the work of Christ in Augustine's life. The first section moves from Augustine's birth to his rebirth with a "new will" in Christ, ending with the death of his

Christian mother, Monica. The second section is an examination of the inner world and the outer world, with a perceptive study of memory and time. The book follows the pattern of Augustine's life. After his conversion he sought to understand all of God's creation with his new will. *Confessions* describes his self-examination as a Christian and reflects a clear biblical understanding of human nature and fallenness. Augustine elevates the grace of the gospel and finds God's grace acting in his own life. He criticizes the Neoplatonists for their pride: They missed the "way to God" by not yielding to the humility of the Incarnation; it is the humble Jesus who lifts up those who cast themselves upon him.

Almost equally well known is Augustine's treatise *City of God*. In 410 refugees streamed into North Africa as a result of the Fall of Rome. They demanded an answer from Augustine as to why God would allow such a catastrophe to occur. *City of God* attempted to resolve such questions.

Although the complete work (twenty-two books) took twenty-two years to complete, the crisis in Rome made early circulation of the first three books necessary. In the first book Augustine addresses the crisis in Rome by showing that the barbarian king Alaric had recognized Christian churches as sanctuaries and that those who fled there were spared; this clemency was not practiced by pagan Rome. He also recalled calamities that had come to the Romans during the Punic wars in the pre-Christian period when only the pagan gods were supposed to be protecting them. Augustine also suggested that Christians suffered along with pagans in the city of Rome in order to teach them not to love the present world and to focus instead on eternal life.

Actually, Augustine devoted only a small part of *City of God* to the crisis in Rome. His primary concern was condemning paganism as the root of human evil—it reflected human pride. Augustine saw Rome as being "ruled by the lust to rule." According to Augustine, Rome was usurping the authority of God. Augustine continued his attack on pagan pride through book ten, delving into such topics as religion, philosophy, and history as well.

In the second half of *City of God* (books 11–22), Augustine traces the history of two cities, the city of earth and the city of God, from their origins to their destinies at the final judgment. In this history, he attempts a theological answer to every possible question that could be raised by both pagans and Christians. The city of earth, which at its root is the city of pride, had its origin in the pride and evil will of Satan. This pride entered into human hearts when Adam and Eve desired to be as God. The origin of the city of God is found in God himself, and the only way to that city is through Jesus Christ, the God-man. Beginning with Cain and Abel, Augustine used historical parallels and "types" to point ahead to Christ as the fulfillment of events and prophecy. With historical parallels, he illustrated the two cities through all periods of time.

City of God assumes a biblical (linear) approach to history: God began the events in creation, controls them by his will, and will eventually bring them to an end. In contrast, pagan histories often viewed events as part of some great cycle with no definite beginning or end. *City of God* does not address the idea of a "Christian state." Even when Augustine wrote about the Christian emperor Theodosius, he merely praised him for his Christian deeds and piety. Augustine said that God gives the possession of empires to good and bad alike according to his will.

Rule of Saint Benedict c. 540
Benedict of Nursia

. . . .

Benedict was born in Nursia, a small town in the middle of Italy. While pursuing his education in rhetoric and law at Rome, Benedict became repulsed by the immorality he found there. He left Rome before finishing his studies and went off to live in a cave near Subiaco. Eventually Benedict became the abbot for a group of monks near the area. After a short while, however, he was asked to leave because the monks there resented his strictness. Returning a second time, Benedict was again forced to leave because of a jealous priest. Around 520 he established a monastery at Monte Cassino, where he stayed until his death. It was here that Benedict drew up his *Rule.*

The *Rule of Saint Benedict* is composed of a prologue and seventy-three chapters. Benedict compiled and modified his *Rule* from a variety of earlier rules and practices of other monastic communities. Through simple, direct language, Benedict expanded on these earlier rules, augmenting them with his own understanding derived from experience. He devised a balanced and flexible system for bringing order to monastic communities and giving meaning to everyday life experiences. According to Benedict, if order and meaning could be established, the higher attributes of wisdom and virtue could also be attained.

Benedict's *Rule* can be considered a monastic directory of operations that is both spiritual and practical. The *Rule* addresses primarily daily activities and concerns of the monastery: meals, work, clothing, travel, worship, etc. It prescribes a balance of prayer, work, and study and calls for strict adherence to poverty, chastity, and obedience. The *Rule* is characterized by moderation, sensibility, and humanity. Benedict believed that such common concerns, rightly accomplished, could lead to perfection. Benedict was opposed to the extreme ascetic practices of some monks. Instead, he sought to create an environment where believers could pursue the service of God and their own spiritual improvement through a balanced life of manual labor, reading, prayer, and worship.

According to the *Rule,* a monk's relationship with God is mirrored in his relationship with the abbot of the monastery, as well as with the other monks of the community. Those called to the monastic life share all things in common, forgive offenses, and live in compassion for others' weaknesses. Allowances are made in the *Rule* for individual differences, such as age, capability, disposition, needs, spiritual maturity, and weaknesses. The broad and simple spirituality of the *Rule* makes it adaptable to various local traditions.

Overall, the *Rule* challenges the individual to become empty of self-interest and self-will and to live in trust of God's mercy rather than in anxious fear. Such emptiness and trust are characteristics of the perfect life of love.

Although there is no evidence that Benedict originally intended to found an entire order of monks, he did intend for his *Rule* to be followed in monasteries all over Europe and Asia. Benedict's hopes for a broad range of readership can be seen in the considerations he makes for certain rules, such as the allowances he makes for clothing styles because of differences in climate.

The legacies of Benedict's *Rule* are numerous. These included the practice of a one-year probation for new members; the life-time election of the abbot; and the function of officials, such as prior, steward, novice master, guest master, etc. Benedict forbade the ownership of even the smallest item and ordained that silence should prevail in the monastery. Monastic bodies have drawn upon the spiritual treasury of the *Rule of Saint Benedict* for centuries, and other institutions have benefited from its wisdom as well.

Cur Deus Homo? (Why Did God Become Human?)   1099
Anselm of Canterbury

Born in Aosta (northwest Italy) to a wealthy family, Anselm was educated at the abbey of Saint Leger. The classical education he received there would later become very evident through the clarity of expression found throughout his writings. Anselm's father had envisioned a political career for his son and opposed

Anselm's decision to become a monk. In 1057 Anselm left home and traveled in Burgundy and Normandy (France) for two years before settling in a Benedictine monastery at Bec, Normandy. There he studied under the renowned theologian Lanfranc. Eventually, Anselm took monastic vows and succeeded his teacher as prior in 1063. He later became abbot of Bec (1078–1093). Under Anselm's leadership, the monastery and its school became a prominent center of learning. Although he was renowned for his scathing condemnations of monks who laid up treasure on earth, Anselm could also show compassion for ordinary human weakness.

After the Norman conquest of England in 1066, English lands were granted by William I to the monastery of Bec. During his three visits to this property in England, Anselm made a favorable impression on the clergy there. When the archbishopric of Canterbury became vacant on Lanfranc's death in 1089, the English clergy urged that Anselm should succeed him. For the gentle monk it was not an inviting prospect. The new English king, William II, was reluctant to appoint anyone to the vacant office, since the revenues of any vacant diocese went to the Crown. After four years of vacancy, however, Anselm was called to hear the confession of the king, who had become seriously ill; the king then pressed Anselm to accept the office of archbishop.

Anselm refused to accept the position until William restored certain lands to Canterbury, recognized the archbishop as his spiritual father, and acknowledged Urban II as the rightful pope. The king agreed but would later disregard his promises. Anselm and William II proved to be incompatible. Again and again William undermined Anselm's administration of the church. The king would not even permit the archbishop to go on a visit to Rome. Anselm refused to dilute his principles to satisfy a royal tyrant, and he eventually left the country in 1097. He returned only upon invitation after William II had died (1100).

As a scholar, Anselm reintroduced the spirit of Augustine into theology. Much of Anselm's writing was done during the placid decades at the monastery at Bec. Anselm tried to demonstrate the existence and attributes of God by appealing to reason alone. He spoke of an absolute norm above time and space that could be comprehended by human minds. This norm was God, the ultimate standard of perfection. Anselm developed what has since been called the ontological argument for the existence of God. Basically this argument asserts that existence of the idea of God necessarily implies the objective existence of God. Anselm always insisted, however, that faith must precede reason.

Anselm is also credited with the "satisfaction theory" of atonement, which sees human sinfulness as an offense to God, for which the offenders, the human race, must somehow make restitution. This was done through the sacrifice of the God-man, Jesus Christ. This view is elaborated in Anselm's famous work *Cur Deus Homo?* which Anselm completed in 1099 in Italy. He rejected the view of the "ransom theory" of atonement, which understood Christ's sacrifice as a payment by God for lost humanity.

Acknowledged as the greatest scholar between Augustine and Aquinas, Anselm's distinctive characteristic is his emphasis upon intellectual reasoning in the realm of theology. At the same time, however, faith was of prime importance to Anselm. He has often been labeled the father of Scholasticism. His theology has had a profound influence on many later theologians, including Karl Barth.

Cur Deus Homo? is often considered Anselm's foremost contribution to theology. This work explores the reasons for the Incarnation and considers the "satisfaction theory" of atonement. Anselm believed that the human race, through sin, has committed a dreadful offense against God and his honor. Humankind marred God's perfect workmanship by refusing righteousness.

As a result of this offense, humankind must make compensation, or satisfaction, for such an injury to God's honor, and the satisfaction must be proportional to the weight of the offense as well as to the status of the offended party. Since God is infinite, humankind can never make total satisfaction by its own power, and eternal death is inevitable. In order to save his honor, however, the infinite God himself provided the necessary compensation for the offense made against him by human sinfulness. This is why God became human and made compensation for sin by his death.

Some critics accuse Anselm's theory of depending too heavily upon feudal justice with its insistence that satisfaction be made in proportion to the offended party's social status. Others emphasize the influence of Roman law upon Anselm's conception of God and his nature. Still others say that the system of repentance in the medieval church influenced Anselm's thinking. This system involved a scale of merits and penance that were proportional to the weight of the sin. Despite these criticisms, Anselm's "satisfaction theory" continues to be recognized as a significant system for explaining the Christian concept of atonement.

Sermons on the Song of Songs c. 1135
Bernard of Clairvaux
. . . .

Bernard was born into nobility at Fontaines in eastern France (1090). He entered the abbey of Citeaux (France) in 1113, and two years later he selected Clairvaux as the location to found a new monastery. He spent much of the rest of his life at this remote monastery, continually struggling to balance the life of ascetic retirement with Christian involvement in the world.

The quality and devotion of every Christian's spiritual walk became Bernard's primary focus. He pictured the ideal Christian life as a separation of soul and body, an emptying of worldly desire, and a final union of the soul with God. In his book *Twelve Steps to Humility,* Bernard attempts to harmonize the divine and human wills without confusing the essential differences between the two.

Bernard's views regarding mystical contemplation often brought him into conflict with scholars at the universities who assumed a more philosophical approach to truth. Peter Abelard often attacked Bernard's beliefs that the highest truth, God, could be obtained by mystical contemplation, and Bernard likewise challenged Abelard and others for their reliance upon worldly reason and the mind.

Bernard supported the second Crusade in 1149 with great enthusiasm and convinced kings to "take up the cross" for this enterprise. Bernard also launched an evangelistic mission to university students in Paris and southern France, in hopes of limiting heresy in those areas.

Highly respected in his own day for his saintliness, austerity, and personal charm, Bernard of Clairvaux has continued to influence the church through his writings. He is often considered the greatest master of language in the Middle Ages. Among the hymns attributed to him are "Jesus, the Very Thought of Thee" and "O Sacred Head Now Wounded." He also wrote many sermons, devotional treatises, and commentaries. His mysticism, well stated and positive, was based solely on the love of God. Although other Christian mystics had already said many of the same things, Bernard was able to communicate them much more effectively. Bernard's zeal produced a certain bluntness of communication and a seemingly uncharitable attitude at times, but his commitment to God and the church was unquestioned.

"Be ready to eat not milk but bread. In Solomon there is bread, and bread that is fine and flavorsome; I speak of the book which is called the Song of Songs. Let it be brought forth, then, if you please, and broken." In 1135 Bernard of Clairvaux began his *Sermons on the Song of Songs* with these words. He continued to preach on this small book, with occasional interruptions, for eighteen years until his death in 1153. Bernard related the Song of Songs to everything from current affairs to personal experiences. But Bernard's most notable reflections address what he believed was the climax of the spiritual journey: the mystical union of love between the believer and God. This topic became the dominant theme in all Bernard's writings.

Bernard's passionate mysticism is immediately evident in his *Sermons on Song of Songs,* as he comments on 1:2: "His living and effective word is a kiss, not a meeting of lips, which can sometimes be deceptive about the state of the heart, but a full infusion of joys, a revelation of secrets, a wonderful and inseparable mingling of the light from above and the mind on which it is shed." Bernard's spirituality is not completely ethereal, however; rather, it is based on experience. Bernard often speaks of personal experience throughout the book: "Only the touch of the Holy Spirit teaches, and it is learned by experience alone. Let those who have experienced it enjoy it; let those who have not, burn with desire, not so much to know it as to experience it"; and "It is my duty to speak and I may not be silent; my words stem from my own experience or from that of others."

For Bernard, the Song of Songs is a great allegory of the loving relationship between the soul and God. The narrator relates the thoughts of the soul, while the bridegroom represents God. The bride and bridegroom "share one inheritance, one table, one house, one bed, one flesh." Such cohesion is not created by human effort; it is the result of divine grace. The allegorical bride carries a second meaning as well—she represents the church, the community of believers that shares the divine love of the Bridegroom. Bernard notes Paul's words regarding marriage, "This is a great mystery, but it is an illustration of the way Christ and the church are one" (Ephesians 5:32).

Bernard develops his thoughts about good works in light of this mystical union between the soul and God. Since this union is not simply personal but involves the church, "once [the loving soul] has tasted . . . the delights of contemplation, it joyfully dedicates itself to new works." Bernard believed that the soul fluctuated between contemplation and action and that the "heart quickly returns to contemplation, as to the source of good works."

Journey of the Soul to God   c. 1259
Bonaventura
. . . .

Born Giovanni Fidanza of Bagnoregio in Tuscany, Bonaventura became one of the most outstanding minds of the Middle Ages. He has been called the second founder of the Franciscan order, which he joined about 1238. He studied under Alexander of Hales at Paris, and from 1248 to 1255 he taught theology there. He then became the general, or head, of the Franciscans.

Bonaventura regarded theology as the basis for understanding what was believed. Faith and reason were brought together and made compatible by love. Like Augustine and Anselm, he said, "I believe in order to understand." For Bonaventura, reason or nature alone cannot lead one to God, although they display God's glory. Human knowledge is dependent on divine knowledge and truth, which are gifts of God's grace.

An important aspect of Bonaventura's mystical theology is the primacy of the will. Purification of the will precedes salvation; only after this can the new believer develop through personal experience. Bonaventura's mysticism has been described as more joyful, less doctrinal, and less cloistered than the mysticism of others before him.

In addition to his theological achievements and his reputation as a man of piety, Bonaventura demonstrated considerable administrative ability. He helped to develop his order's constitution by his commentary on the rule of Saint Francis and by his biography of the founder. He tried to bring together diverse elements that had arisen among the Franciscans. As head of the order, Bonaventura became an opponent of Thomas Aquinas, the most influential thinker during the Middle Ages. The two differed in their understanding of how spiritual truth can be known. Many later theologians tended to appeal to Bonaventura, whose ideas more closely resembled Augustine and the Protestant reformers.

Bonaventura's masterpiece, *Journey of the Soul to God,* is a synthesis of the author's mysticism and theology. It shows the way humans should love and contemplate God through Christ, following the example of Saint Francis.

This short book is a system of metaphysics through which the soul ascends to God through a series of stages or steps. Bonaventura posits that the human soul has three aspects, each of which is twofold: (1) a body, which has animality or sensuality; (2) a spirit, which looks inward; and (3) a mind, which looks above. This view of the soul produces six stages for the believer to ascend to God. These stages lead from the lower, external, and temporal to the higher, internal, and eternal. The soul uses the powers of sense, imagination, reason, intellect, intelligence, and illumination of conscience to mount these steps to God.

In the first stage, the soul recognizes God's power and excellence in the visible creation. Second, the soul contemplates God and the invisible things of God by extrapolating from knowledge gained by the five senses. This contemplation is possible because God is the origin and end of every created thing. In the third stage, the eye of reason is able to see the divine image shining in the mirror of the mind.

In the fourth stage, the believer turns from the world that is perceived through the senses and turns to the image of God within the soul. This turn is made possible through faith in Jesus Christ, through the gifts of grace, and through faith, hope, and love. During this stage, the mind becomes the temple of the Holy Spirit, who reveals the secrets of God.

In the fifth stage of Bonaventura's system, the soul continues its ascent to God by contemplating God's essential attributes. Bonaventura calls the contemplation of these attributes *Being.* God's attributes include omnipotence, omniscience, and goodness. To see these perfectly is to be blessed.

The final stage is the soul's contemplation of the invisible and eternal things of God—the properties of the persons of God in the Trinity. Bonaventura names this stage *Good,* and in it the soul sees not only the essential and personal traits of God but also the unity of God and humanity in Christ. Here the stages reach perfection; all intellectual operations are abandoned. This revelation of mystic wisdom is only given by the Holy Spirit. In it the soul's entire affection is mystically and secretly transferred into God.

Summa Theologica 1273
Thomas Aquinas

Thomas was born into nobility in the Italian town of Aquino, about eighty miles southeast of Rome. As a child, Thomas (also referred to as "Aquinas") had a large physique that earned him the nickname "dumb ox." His combination of theological learning and Christian devotion, however, would later earn him the title "angelic doctor." When he was five, Thomas's parents sent him to the Benedictine school at Monte Cassino in hopes that he would eventually become an abbot.

At the age of fifteen, while attending the University of Naples, Thomas sought admission to the newly founded Dominican order. His parents opposed this intention and confined him to their home for fifteen months. Thomas was determined, however, and joined the Dominican order in 1244. Later he would study at Paris, where he was introduced to the writings of Aristotle, and then he moved to Cologne. Soon after his studies, Thomas Aquinas began lecturing in theology and philosophy at various universities, and he wrote an immense number of books on these subjects, including his mammoth works *Summa Theologica* and *Summa Contra Gentiles.*

The theologians of Aquinas's day so distrusted his use of Aristotelian philosophy that some of his teachings were condemned by the church for about fifty years. But his cause was soon taken up by the entire Dominican order, which adopted his theology (known as Thomism); the Franciscan monks followed the teachings of Bonaventura and Duns Scotus instead. Over the centuries, however, the teachings of Thomas Aquinas significantly influenced the Roman Catholic Church. Although Thomism is not the official Catholic position, Aquinas is held in the highest respect, is diligently studied, and has had a profoundly stabilizing effect on Catholic thought throughout the centuries.

Aquinas is often criticized by Protestants because he attempted a synthesis of Aristotelian philosophy and biblical theology that, in the judgment of some, compromised such doctrines as the sovereignty of God and the total depravity of humankind. Many contend that Aquinas was mistaken in his assumption that fallen human beings can still accurately perceive universal truth through reason. Aquinas, on the other hand, argued that it is the will, not the intellect, that is fallen. Aquinas's theological and philosophical system is the most developed example of what has since been called "natural theology."

Summa Theologica was written as a theology textbook for undergraduates. It is an encyclopedic statement of Aquinas's teachings, meticulously developed and defended with replies to objections from both Christian and non-Christian authorities.

Written between 1265 and 1273, it provides a systematic summary of all theological, philosophical, and ethical topics debated in medieval universities. Many of these summaries have become classic statements on such topics as the relation of theology to philosophy, the arguments for God's existence, and the doctrines of creation, natural law, ethics, etc.

The work's organization reflects the Scholastic method of Aquinas's day: Each question is divided into several subquestions known as "articles." Each article is introduced with objections to a standard position, followed by Aquinas's own arguments, which begin "I answer that . . ." Throughout this process, Aquinas not only argues from Scripture but also considers the opinions of various Christian and non-Christian authorities, reflecting his convictions about the role of reason in theology.

Aquinas divides theology into three major areas: (1) God (including his relationship to creation); (2) humanity (including its relationship to God's law and to grace); and (3) Christ (including his person and work, his sacraments, and his church). A fourth section on the Sacraments and the Last Things was begun, but Aquinas died before its completion.

One of the more famous arguments found in *Summa Theologica* is Aquinas's "five ways" for proving the existence of God, based on what humans are able to perceive around them. In the first of these five arguments, Aquinas observes that every natural process of change actualizes some potential. Firewood is potentially hot, but it actually becomes hot when it burns; yet it is not both potentially and actually hot at the same time. The universal truth here is that whatever is changed or moved must be changed or moved by another. But an infinite chain of movers is impossible, for without a "first mover" there could be no first movement or change. Therefore, a first mover, itself moved by nothing else, must exist—namely an unchanging God.

Second, Aquinas observed in nature a seemingly endless array of cause-effect relationships, or "efficient causes" in his Aristotelian terminology. But that array is not actually endless, for nothing can be its own cause, as the whole causal order would be if it were actually endless. Therefore, a first efficient cause of the whole array of causes must be admitted, namely God.

Third, Aquinas notes that nature exhibits a large variety of possibilities, things that are created and destroyed and therefore do not have to exist. But if all that exists could possibly not exist, then at one point in an endless time past nothing at all could have existed, and consequently nothing would now exist. There must therefore exist some being whose existence is not merely possible but necessary by virtue of his very nature. That necessary being is God.

The fourth way observes varying degrees of goodness, beauty, truth, and so forth in different things, each according to the form of its own species. This hierarchy of being and goodness implies that something must exist that is best, most beautiful, truest, and most real. That something is, in fact, the God who is perfect in all his attributes.

The fifth and final way starts from the fact that even unthinking things follow natural and preestablished tendencies as if they are deliberately pursuing some good end. But things do not pursue ends unless they are intelligent or else are guided by an intelligent being. Therefore, some intelligent being exists who draws all things to those ends, namely, the God who works his purposes in and through the things he made.

The first three "ways" argue from the dependent existence of finite things to the independent existence of God and are varieties of the so-called cosmological argument. Aquinas's remaining two ways begin with order and purpose in nature and are variations of the "teleological argument," as it was later called.

Summa Theologica addresses many other theological and philosophical topics besides the existence of God and the nature of

human reason. The enormous impact of this work, combined
with Aquinas's dependence upon Aristotle and other classical
philosophers, led to a noticeable synthesis of classical philosophy with later Christian thought.

Divine Comedy   c. 1315
Dante Alighieri
. . . .

In 1265 Dante Alighieri, probably the most eminent Italian
writer in history, was born to a noble family in Florence. He was
educated under the supervision of the Dominican and Franciscan
orders. As a young man, he was made one of the priors (chief
magistrates) of the Florentine republic and entered into the political struggles that divided Florence into several hostile factions.
While absent on a diplomatic mission in 1302, he was exiled
from Florence. Some thirteen years afterward, he was invited to
return to his native city if he would submit to certain humiliating
conditions. Dante refused. He spent the rest of his life in exile in
various Italian cities, including Verona, Padua, and Bologna, and
died in Ravenna in 1321.

Dante's first significant work was *La Vita Nuova,* written between 1292 and 1295. Composed partly in blank verse and partly
in prose, the book tells of Dante's love for a lady named Beatrice
and promises to treat the subject more worthily later. Dante ful-
filled this promise in the *Divine Comedy,* a three-book poem
begun early in his exile and completed shortly before his death.
Beatrice Portinari, the object of the poet's idealized love, hardly
knew Dante at all. He had met her only briefly when he was nine
years old and once again at age eighteen.

Dante's work *De Monarchia* was declared heretical by the
church. This work, written in exile about 1312, is a political treatise in which Dante defends the emperor's supremacy in temporal matters over the authority of the church. Dante put forward

the idea of a single world government that would secure universal peace, thus promoting the full realization of humanity's intellectual and cultural potential.

Dante Alighieri begins his epic poem the *Divine Comedy* as a traveler in a dark woods at Easter in 1300. In the first book, entitled the *Inferno,* he is led by the Roman poet Virgil down into the various stages of hell. Along the way he encounters various figures from history (many of whom were leaders in the church) who are being punished in various ways, depending upon the nature of their sins. In the *Purgatorio,* Virgil continues to lead Dante up a mountain rising from the ocean shore. Dante eventually reaches a point high above earth, the "earthly paradise." The *Paradiso* then takes up the story, and Virgil is replaced by the idealized woman Beatrice, who leads him by the loving power of her glancing eye through the revolving ten heavens and into the presence of God. Dante writes of this sight as a glimpse of the "Beatific Vision." The *Inferno* may be considered the prologue of the *Divine Comedy,* the *Purgatorio* its development, and, as the final vision of Dante's experience, the *Paradiso* forms the poem's conclusion and resolution.

Dante originally titled his work *Commedia,* indicating the pleasing end of the poem. It was only later that its admirers expanded the title to the *Divine Comedy* because of the poem's lofty subject. Dante's purpose in writing the *Commedia* was "to remove those living in this life from the state of misery and lead them to the state of happiness."

This epic poem is composed in *terza rima,* a rhyme scheme of aba/bcb/cdc/ and so on. Its 14,233 lines contain eleven syllables each (a hendecasyllable), and the lines are organized into 100 *cantos* of 142 lines. Each *canto* is divided into three *cantica* of 33 lines each. One *canto* serves as a prologue to the entire work. Dante wrote in vernacular Italian, a transitional language between Latin and modern Italian.

Inspired by the poetry of the Bible, and following the tradition of medieval allegorical poetry, Dante modeled the *Commedia* on Virgil's *Aeneid*. Superficially, the *Commedia* belongs to the medieval literary types of the journey and the vision. In a deeper sense, the symbolism of the journey's stages and Dante's experiences along the way make the *Commedia* an allegory of the history of a human soul. The poem is also an encyclopedia of Dante's knowledge of theology, philosophy, astronomy, cosmology, and other areas of learning. Contemporaneous poetry was often written in praise of women. But Dante eclipsed all such poetry by making the *Commedia* a monument to Beatrice, a symbolic figure developed from a person Dante first saw when a child and later loved as the ideal of womanhood. With all this, the *Commedia* is also an autobiography, not of outward events, but of the struggles of Dante's inner life.

In Dante's allegorical world, the sages of pagan antiquity have their eternal dwelling in Limbo. When passing this place, Virgil introduces Dante to Homer, Horace, Ovid, and Lucan. They receive him with honor as "a sixth among such intelligences." In this way Dante boldly predicts the judgment of future generations: The *Commedia* sums up an entire era of human history—the Middle Ages. While doing so, it outstrips that era's literature, philosophy, science, religion, and language and is itself the rebirth of European poetry. For these reasons, it is only appropriate that Dante's *Commedia* be labeled "divine."

Revelations of Divine Love   1393
Julian of Norwich

Almost nothing factual is known about Julian, but tradition associates her with Saint Julian's church, Norwich, which is near the place where Julian lived a solitary life of prayer and meditation. She is also known by many as Mother Julian or Lady Julian. In

May of 1373, when Julian was about thirty years old, she became sick and seemed to be near death for six days. On the seventh day, fifteen revelations, or "showings," began that lasted nearly twelve hours. The next day she received the final vision: Her soul appeared to her as a city, an endless world, and a blessed kingdom with Christ sitting in it.

Julian meditated on these visions for twenty years, concentrating on the love of God, which supplies the answer to all life's problems and to the evil in the world. Eventually she wrote the first English literary work written by a woman: *Revelations of Divine Love.*

Revelations of Divine Love is a record of Julian's original visions and her meditations on them. The times of Julian of Norwich were devastated by the Hundred Years War, the Black Death, and social and religious upheaval. Against this background, the author produced a lucid work of Christian mysticism.

Julian relates that as a young woman she prayed that she would (1) have the knowledge of Christ's suffering; (2) experience serious sickness in order to know the suffering of dying without actually entering death; and (3) receive three wounds: the wounds of true repentance, of kind compassion, and of longing for God. Through sickness and her visions, Julian was able to fulfill these desires. The first twelve visions focus on Christ's crucifixion. The pain of these visions was nearly impossible for Julian to endure, but she refused the temptation to look away. Through these visions, Julian came to believe that in their present lives believers are "on [Christ's] cross dying with him in our pains and our passion."

Julian's questions about sin and pain were answered by Christ in her visions. She learned that God sends suffering to his children, not because they have offended him, but to prepare their souls for greater bliss. True to the best of Christian mysticism,

Revelations of Divine Love maintains a tension between the pain and sin of human life and the love and bliss of the divine.

Julian also stresses the "motherhood" of Christ in her *Revelations.* She was not the first to mention this concept. Other writers, including Anselm of Canterbury, had previously written of Christ's "motherhood," but Julian was the first to list it among the three roles of God: father, mother, and lord. For Julian, God is a father because Christians have their being from him; he is a mother in the mercy he shows; and he is the Lord in the grace he gives.

Some scholars hold that Julian of Norwich was influenced by a famous book on mystical experience, *The Cloud of Unknowing,* as well as by Neoplatonic philosophy. Regardless, she has remained a favorite source for mystical contemplation for many Christians throughout the ages.

Imitation of Christ   c. 1418
Thomas à Kempis
. . . .

Thomas Hemerken was born in 1380 in Kempen (from which he derived his more popular name), a town in the Rhine valley not far from Cologne. He was the younger of two sons in a peasant family. In 1392 Thomas entered the famous cathedral school at Deventer, a town in the Yssel valley in what is now the Netherlands.

Through his older brother, John, who had earlier gone to Windesheim, near Deventer, Thomas came into contact with Florens Radewijns, a highly respected member of the Brethren of the Common Life and a famous preacher. Thomas was not wealthy and was unable to pay for his board and lodging, so Radewijns invited him to stay at his house. Radewijns provided him with books and paid his tuition at the school of Saint Lebwin. Radewijns's support of Thomas was typical among members of the Brethren of the Common Life, who aided and educated many poor youth. Later, Thomas seems to have lived with some other Brethren in a house at Deventer. He wrote about this time: "All I earned, I gave to the community. Here I learned to read and write the Holy Scriptures and books on moral subjects, but it was chiefly through the sweet conversation of the Brethren that I was inspired yet more strongly to despise the world. I took pleasure in their godly conduct."

About 1399 Thomas à Kempis went to Mount Saint Agnes, a newly founded monastery of the Canons Regular of Saint Augustine. He was ordained a priest about 1413 and spent the remainder of his life there, except for a brief period when the community moved. He was subprior in 1425 and again in 1448. Other monks were greatly impressed with his great religious fervor. By the time he died, his name had made the monastery of Mount Saint Agnes well known.

Thomas copied many manuscripts, a primary activity of the Brethren. He wrote devotional works, sermons, and chronicles. Many of his works address the topics of poverty, humility, and chastity. There are sermons to novices and a number of biographies of saints. The principal work for which Thomas is known is the *Imitation of Christ,* a classic devotional.

Thomas's life and work are the best-known examples of the religious renewal brought about by the Brethren of the Common Life. Thomas and his fellow workers did much to raise the level of religious awareness in the Low Countries, both through their work with the general laity and through reform of existing religious institutions, such as monasteries and convents. Although the Brethren did not actively join in the Protestant Reformation, their work undoubtedly contributed much to the vast success of the Reformation in the Low Countries.

Imitation of Christ is a product of the Brethren of the Common Life, a group that arose in Holland at the end of the fourteenth century. Primarily concerned with the care and education of Dutch youth, the group emphasized the revival of religious life and the active following of Christ by each individual believer. Thomas à Kempis edited and published *Imitation of Christ* from a religious house run by the Brethren.

Imitation of Christ is a manual of spiritual advice to help believers follow Christ's example. The book contains four parts, with the first two sections containing general counsel for the spiritual life. The third section explores the inner life of the soul, and the fourth addresses the sacrament of Holy Communion.

For Thomas, in order to fully understand the words of Christ, the Christian must strive to conform to the life of Christ. This requires the believer to follow Christ in the way of the cross as well. By this, Thomas meant the believer must be content with suffering and hardship, "for only the servants of the cross can find the way of blessedness and of true light." Once a believer begins this journey, however, there is no turning back. Thomas lamented that the cause of shame in a Christian was the failure to pursue this goal of imitating Christ.

Imitation of Christ also emphasizes the importance of listening to the gentle voice of the Holy Spirit. This inner voice is vital to anyone seeking to imitate Christ. It is dramatically contrasted with the speaking of the prophets of the Old Testament: "Let not Moses speak unto me, nor any of the prophets, but rather do thou speak, O Lord God, the inspirer and enlightener of all the prophets." In order to hear this voice, the believer should also develop a disciplined habit of prayer and meditation.

Thomas portrays humanity as entirely incapable of progressing by its own merit in the holiness described in *Imitation of Christ*. He asserts that "there is no worse enemy, nor one more troublesome to the soul, than thou art to thyself, if thou be not in harmony with the Spirit." He recites a detailed catalog of human

weaknesses and failings and concludes with an admonition to
continually strive toward holiness.

There is great controversy as to the true author of *Imitation of
Christ.* For the most part, contemporary scholars are confident
that, before his early death in 1374, Gerard Groote wrote the text
of *Imitation of Christ.* Thomas à Kempis, though historically
given credit as its author, served more as editor and publisher of
this enduring work.

The Renaissance
and Reformation

Greek New Testament (Textus Receptus)   1516
Erasmus
. . . .

Born out of wedlock to a priest, Erasmus knew little of normal
family life as a child. He received most of his schooling at
Deventer under the auspices of the Brethren of the Common
Life. These followers of what was called the Modern Devotion
movement sought a deepening of spiritual life. Under the
Brethren, who produced some of the fifteenth century's best
teachers, Erasmus acquired an enthusiasm for Bible study. In
1486, evidently under pressure from his guardians, he became an
Augustinian canon at Steyn (Netherlands). In spite of his
reluctance to enter the monastery, Erasmas's six or seven years
of study there cultivated his love for classical literature and
thought.

Around 1493 Erasmus was ordained and became Latin secretary to the bishop of Cambrai, France. The bishop's continuing
interest allowed Erasmus to pursue theological studies at Paris in
1495. Erasmus developed a lasting dislike for the dogmatic theologians there, with their partisanship, intolerance, and hostility to
new ways of thinking.

In 1496, after a brief visit to Steyn, Erasmus returned to Paris. By now he had become determined to leave the monastic life. He continued his theological studies but majored in the new biblical courses rather than in Scholastic theology. Meanwhile, Erasmus helped to support himself by tutoring the sons of leading European families. During this time he wrote his *Colloquies,* a series of imaginary dialogues that satirized Scholasticism and monkish superstition.

In 1499 Erasmus paid his first visit to England. He met several prominent churchmen there, including Bishop Warham of London, John Fisher, William Latimer, John Colet, and Thomas More. The last two exercised a profound influence upon Erasmus. In England Erasmus also rekindled his passion for classical learning. He wanted to develop a distinctly Christian character for classical learning instead of allowing Europe to return to pagan values in the wake of the Renaissance. He found support for this wish in England, especially from people like John Colet, who encouraged Erasmus in the study of the New Testament.

In 1500 Erasmus left England and went to Paris and then to Louvain, Belgium. In 1505 and 1506 Erasmus revisited England and then went to Italy, receiving his doctorate at Turin. In Italy, Erasmus saw much corruption surrounding the papacy. Upon the accession of Henry VIII to the English throne in 1509, Erasmus returned to England for five years. He stayed for a time with Thomas More and wrote the *Encomium moriae,* which was later translated into English as *The Praise of Folly.* The book was a biting satire on monastic and ecclesiastical corruption, on the many supposed miracles wrought by images, on the scandal of indulgences, on useless rites, and on the papal hierarchy. This work significantly helped to prepare the way for the Reformation.

Erasmus also criticized Scholasticism for its inordinate preoccupation with details and its ignorance of true religion. He pointed to the early church and to the church fathers as the ideal of reform rather than to the complex argumentations of later Scholastics. The test of true theology, Erasmus claimed, was its reflection in Christian living.

Before the church could return to first-century Christianity, Erasmus thought, people must know what kind of Christianity that was. So in 1516 he published the most noted work of his life: an edition of the Greek New Testament text. In a parallel column he also printed his own elegant Latin version with critical notes. His own Latin translation occasionally conflicted with the Vulgate text, setting in motion a new era of revision and reconstruction in biblical studies. The work was dedicated to Pope Leo X and was hailed with delight by Martin Luther. This was only one year before Luther defied the pope by posting his Ninety-five Theses on the church door in Wittenberg.

In 1516 Erasmus became a royal counselor in the Brussels court of the future Holy Roman Emperor Charles V. Around 1518 Erasmus also published a nine-volume edition of the works of Jerome, his favorite church father. Less ambitious editions of other fathers, including Irenaeus, Augustine, Chrysostom, and Origen, followed in the succeeding eighteen years.

In 1521 Erasmus settled at Basel, Switzerland, a city he found most satisfying for his work. There he published many books and continued his "back to the fathers" movement. Although several friends in high places offered him various posts, Erasmus declined them all in order to maintain his literary freedom. Erasmus continued to assail long-entrenched evils in the church, but he toned down his attack just when papal defenses were beginning to crumble before the Reformers' criticisms. Despite appeals from both sides, Erasmus was reluctant to become embroiled in the controversy between Luther and the papacy.

At last, however, in 1524 Erasmus yielded to pressure and attacked Luther with a *Diatribe on Free Will*, to which Luther replied with *Bondage of the Will* (1526). Erasmus came back with *Hyperaspistes Diatribes*. So for the last twelve years of his life, Erasmus was associated with the conservative faction, remaining firmly, if sometimes uneasily, in the Catholic Church.

In 1529, after the Reformation had come to Basel comparatively peacefully, Erasmus was among the humanists who left the city. He went to Freiburg, a German city with a young university. Six years later he returned to Basel, although ill, to supervise the printing of his edition of Origen's works. Erasmus died in Basel the following year.

Erasmus was a man of moderation in an age of extremes; he refused to become caught up in the turbulence of the times. Because of this, his reputation was attacked by both sides of the Reformation controversy. The shy, sensitive bachelor often found his scholarly detachment misunderstood. His words were taken out of context and made to serve undesired ends. His views were used to criticize the papacy and to liberalize Henry VIII's divorce. Nevertheless, Erasmus's works have helped the church refocus its attention on the early church.

The Greek New Testament compiled by Erasmus reflects the influence of the Renaissance upon the church as well as upon society. Renewed interest in classical studies encouraged Erasmus to provide the church with the earliest, most accurate copy of the New Testament that could be compiled. In addition, Erasmus believed the first steps to true reform would be made by learning crucial lessons from the Christian past. All this led to the publication of his Greek New Testament.

Erasmus was approached by the well-known publisher Johann Froben during the years of 1514–1515 to produce a manuscript of the Greek New Testament for printing. Erasmus accepted the offer and then sought out Greek manuscripts for the purpose. But he was not able to find a manuscript of the New Testament that was complete, nor could he find any earlier than the twelfth century, so he had to use several manuscripts for various parts of the New Testament. For most of his work he relied upon two manuscripts from the twelfth century—one for the Gospels and another for Acts and the Epistles. For the book of Revelation he used another twelfth-century manuscript, which lacked the last leaf containing the last six verses of Revelation. For this section, as well as for others throughout Revelation where the manuscript was difficult to read, Erasmus used the Latin Vulgate and translated it back into Greek.

Erasmus's first edition was produced in 1516. Though it was not the first Greek New Testament to be printed (the Complutensian Polyglot appeared in 1514), it quickly became the most well known. Erasmus's edition presented the Greek text alongside his own Latin version, which showed many improvements over the Latin Vulgate. Throughout the course of four editions, Erasmus also worked to prune the Greek text of its errors. But it would be difficult, if not impossible, to purify all textual corruptions from the original text using only twelfth-century manuscripts.

Erasmus's edition, with various alterations, became published again and again by different printers. The printer Robert Estienne eventually printed one such edition, which became known as the *Textus Receptus* ("the text received by all," as it says in the preface). This edition became the standard Greek New Testament for several centuries until it was superseded by superior editions compiled from more reliable manuscript evidence. Nonetheless, Erasmus's edition was a milestone in the modern era, releasing the original text of the Scriptures into the hands of the general public and paving the way for the Reformation. Erasmus himself envisioned great things for his text as he wrote in the preface of the Greek New Testament:

> [I wish that the New Testament books] were translated into each and every language so that they might be read and understood not only by Scots and Irishmen, but also by Turks and Saracens. . . . [I wish] that the farmer might sing

snatches of Scripture at his plough and that the weaver might hum phrases of Scripture to the tune of his shuttle, that the traveler might lighten with stories from Scripture the weariness of his journey.

English New Testament   1525
William Tyndale

William Tyndale was born in western England around 1494. Soon after graduating from Oxford in 1515, where he studied the Scriptures in Greek and Hebrew, Tyndale began translating the New Testament into English.

In 1523 Tyndale went to London, seeking a place to continue work on his translation. When the bishop of London would not give him hospitality, he was provided a place by a cloth merchant. Tyndale left England for Germany in 1524 because the English church, which was still under the papal authority of Rome, strongly opposed releasing the Bible into the hands of the laity. Tyndale first settled in Hamburg, Germany, where he became well acquainted with Martin Luther's writings and his German translation of the New Testament. Both Luther and Tyndale used the Greek text compiled by Erasmus as the original text for their translations.

Tyndale completed his translation of the New Testament in 1525. Fifteen thousand copies in six editions were smuggled into England between the years 1525 and 1530. Church authorities confiscated and burned as many copies of Tyndale's translation as they could, but they could not stop the flow of Bibles from Germany into England. Tyndale himself was banned from returning to England, having been declared an outlaw. However, he continued to work abroad—correcting, revising, and reissuing his translation until his final revision appeared in 1535.

After finishing the New Testament, Tyndale began translating the Old Testament from the original Hebrew, but he did not live long enough to complete his task. He did, however, translate the Pentateuch (the first five books of the Old Testament), Jonah, and a few of the historical books.

In May 1535 Tyndale was arrested and imprisoned in a castle near Brussels. While he was in prison, an associate named Miles Coverdale completed an entire Bible in English—based largely on Tyndale's translation of the New Testament and a few Old Testament books. After being in prison for over a year, Tyndale was tried and condemned to death. He was strangled and burned at the stake on October 6, 1536.

Commentary on the Epistle to the Galatians 1535
Martin Luther
. . . .

Born at Eisleben in Saxony (eastern Germany), Luther attended school at Eisleben and at Magdeburg under the Brethren of the Common Life. He then went to the university at Erfurt (1501), where he learned Greek and was influenced by the popular philosophy of Nominalism. Luther earned his B.A. in 1502 and his M.A. in 1505. He had intended to study law, but due to a narrow escape from death by lightning, he changed his mind and became an Augustinian monk in 1506, despite his father's objections.

In the Erfurt monastery, Luther did further theological study and was made a priest in 1507. He transferred to Wittenberg in 1508, where he read for the B.D. (1509) and began to teach moral theology, the *Sentences* of Peter Lombard, and the Holy Scriptures. In the meantime, a visit to Rome opened Luther's eyes to the corruption prevalent among the higher clergy. Returning to Wittenberg, he earned the degree of doctor of theology and was appointed to the chair of biblical studies, which he occupied for the rest of his life. He also became subprior of the Wittenberg house.

Outwardly Luther was building up a successful monastic and academic career, but inwardly he was troubled by a conviction of sin that his diligence in monastery life could not relieve. Luther read widely in Augustine, Tauler, and the German mystics. His biblical reading, especially in preparation for his classes on the Psalms, on Romans, and on Galatians, finally pushed Luther to his famous "tower experience." During this experience, Luther came to realize that God's righteousness in Romans 1 is not a justice that needs to be feared but a positive righteousness that God gives believers in Christ.

Luther might easily have held and taught his new understanding of justification without interference or vital reforming impact. His colleagues at Wittenberg, both on the theological faculty and in the monastery, supported him, and church life went on undisturbed. In 1517, however, Luther became incensed by the crass materialism peddled by John Tetzel, who was offering indulgences justified by crude theology. This offense finally drove Luther to post ninety-five theses for debate on the Wittenberg door on October 31, 1517. When translated and widely circulated, these theses sparked an explosion of antichurch sentiment throughout Europe. Luther's theology could no longer go unnoticed, and he came at once under ecclesiastical pressure.

Luther refused to be silenced, however. He won over many Augustinians at the Heidelberg disputation in 1518 and argued that he was defying no dogmatic definition of the church. When pressed at the Leipzig disputation in 1519, he claimed the supremacy of scriptural authority over all ecclesiastical authority. Continuing his own preaching and teaching, he defended the theses in his *Explanations* and further explained his theology in *Two Kinds of Righteousness*.

When Charles V, the newly elected emperor, stepped up the pressure, Luther responded in 1520 with three powerful works that have come to be called his primary treatises. In the *Address to the German Nobility,* he appealed to the princes to throw off papal oppression. In the *Babylonian Captivity,* he attacked the current sacramental system. In *The Freedom of a Christian,* he put forth the paradox that the Christian is both a free lord, subject to none, and also a servant, subject to all. He also wrote his *Treatise on Good Works* and his *Sermon on the Mass* during this period.

By the middle of 1520 papal patience was at an end, and a bull was drawn up ordering Luther's recantation and the burning of his works. Protected by the elector Frederick, Luther denounced the bull, and the theology faculty solemnly burned a copy at a ceremony on December 10, 1520. Early in 1521 a stronger bull of excommunication was prepared that, if carried out, would have deprived Luther of civil rights and protection. Before its execution Charles V agreed to give Luther the chance to recant at the diet to be held at Worms. Here Luther made his resounding confession before the emperor: "My conscience is captive to the Word of God. . . . Here I stand; I can do no other."

The situation after Worms seemed hardly favorable for positive reform. A majority at the diet decided to apply the papal bull. In order to shield Luther against violence, Frederick arranged his "kidnapping" on the way home and hid him in the safe castle of Wartburg under the guise of George the Knight. Luther seized the opportunity to begin translating the New Testament directly from Greek into simple, idiomatic German. He finished the New Testament in the fall of 1522 and the Old Testament in 1534. The completed Luther Bible proved to be as powerful a force in the German-speaking world as the King James Version became among English speakers.

After returning from Wartburg in 1522, Luther turned his attention to the sphere of worship. The main step here, as with Scripture, was to make the services understandable by putting them in the native tongue. Luther had no wish to cause friction, however, by unnecessary changes in liturgical structure. He produced conservative orders for baptism and for the Mass in 1523. The order of 1526, which included collects, canticles, and a litany, introduced new paraphrases and hymns for congregational use.

During his time in Wartburg, Luther had given much thought to the question of clerical celibacy, and he had written *On Monastic Vows*. After returning to Wittenberg, Luther's reforming work included the dissolution of monasteries and the ending of clerical celibacy. The resources of the monasteries were made available for the relief of the poor, and marriages between former celibates became the order of the day. Luther himself married the former nun Katherine von Bora, and they had six children. Luther continued to live in what had been the Augustinian convent.

Luther clearly saw the need for education among the laity, and he issued an appeal for Christian schools in 1524. He also preached to parents on the duty of sending children to school. Spiritual as well as secular instruction was needed to remedy the ignorance prevalent in the later Middle Ages. To help pastors provide this, Luther composed a Large Catechism in 1528 and then a more popular Small Catechism in 1529. In the latter he gave a simple exposition of the Creed, the Lord's Prayer, the Ten Commandments, and the two sacraments. He also offered forms for confession, morning and evening prayers, and prayer at meals. To supply more able pastors and teachers for the parishes, Luther supported university reforms, especially in the theological faculties.

After the publication of his ninety-five theses, Luther was engaged in unending debate with the Roman Catholic Church. In addition, he soon found himself in disagreement with other reforming groups. Luther was very blunt and outspoken, and he often came into collision with equally militant opponents. These controversies often took on a bitter edge that brought personal alienation and greatly hampered the general movement of reform.

The first problem arose in 1521 when Luther was in Wartburg. A little group from Zwickau, the Zwickau Prophets, came to Wittenberg and caused a great deal of confusion by their preaching. Visiting the city to deal with the issue, Luther preached against the group and later summed up his criticisms in *Against the Heavenly Prophets.*

When peasants began to revolt in 1524, Luther initially sympathized with their demands, attempted mediation, and issued a call for peace. But then the uprisings increased in 1525 and took on a fanatical character. This led Luther to leave his mediatorial role and to call for the ruthless suppression of the rebels in the interests of divinely willed law and order. Although Luther still made a plea for economic justice, his attitude alienated many of the peasants.

At the very same period Luther became entangled in an unfortunate if unavoidable controversy with the humanist scholar and reformer Erasmus. The two had much in common, sharing concerns for scholarship, for opening up the Scriptures, and for doctrinal and practical reform. Nevertheless, they differed sharply in character and theological approach. Under pressure to declare himself either for Luther or against him, Erasmus turned to the important issue of the freedom of the will and published a *Diatribe on Free Will* (1524). To this Luther made a sharp and almost scornful reply in his *Bondage of the Will* (1525). Erasmus came out with a counterreply, but Luther ignored this. Erasmus then aligned himself with the opponents of the Reformation, although still urging reform and maintaining friendly relations with various reformers.

In 1526 a disruptive eucharistic controversy emerged that would eventually split the Lutherans from the South Germans.

Unfortunately, Luther adopted a confrontational style in this debate that did little to win over his opponents. Philip of Hesse tried to reach an agreement at Marburg in 1529, but in the discussions Luther showed from the first a rigidity that doomed the effort to failure. Later, Luther accepted the uneasy concord with Bucer and the South Germans at Wittenberg (1536).

Luther ran into other difficulties as well. He hoped at first that the renewing of the gospel would open the way for the conversion of the Jews; but when this hope was not realized, he made intemperate attacks on the Jews. Philip of Hesse became a serious embarrassment to Luther by his bigamous marriage in 1540. The development of armed religious alliances in the empire also worried Luther, for while he accepted the divine authority of princes and valued their help in practical reformation, he insisted that the gospel does not need to be advanced or defended by military power.

Pressured by ill health and harassed constantly by political and theological problems, Luther tended to display in his last years the less pleasant aspects of his character. His courage increasingly appeared as pugnacity, his bluntness as crudity, and his steadfastness as obstinacy. Instead of mellowing with the years, his opposition to Roman Catholics, radicals, and other reformers became even more bitter. Ironically, Luther's itinerary eventually brought him full circle to the town of his birth, and it was in Eisleben that he died on February 18, 1546.

Martin Luther, a very human figure, had extraordinary gifts. Perhaps his most striking virtue was his versatility. His mastery of the biblical languages went hand in hand with rare theological insight. Luther could see to the heart of theological questions and express himself with astonishing originality and force. Although he never actually organized his theology together into a structured system, he contributed more to real theology than the vast majority of dogmaticians. And, yet, while his works fill many bulky volumes, the words contained in them are vibrant and challenging, for they came not merely from the study or the podium but from life and action.

Luther's *Commentary on the Epistle to the Galatians* is based on a course of lectures he delivered in 1531 at the University of Wittenberg, where he was professor of biblical exegesis. Galatians was one of Luther's favorite books; he called it "my own epistle" and "my Katie von Bora" (his wife). The enduring effect of his *Commentary* testifies to Luther's passion for the epistle. John Bunyan preferred Luther's *Commentary* to any other book except the Bible.

The *Commentary* consists of an introduction and six chapters; each chapter of Galatians is covered by one chapter of Luther's *Commentary*. The introduction spells out the purpose of the Epistle to the Galatians: "to establish the doctrine of faith, grace, forgiveness of sins, or Christian righteousness." Luther insisted, as in all his works, that Christians receive grace purely through faith, not through any deeds.

The rest of the *Commentary* examines each chapter of Galatians, continually emphasizing Luther's classic theme of justification by faith. Galatians contains a verse that may very well be called the linchpin of Luther's revolutionary doctrine of grace: "Abraham believed God, so God declared him righteous because of his faith" (3:6). One English edition of Luther's *Commentary* included nine pages for Luther's explanation of this verse.

Augsburg Confession 1530
. . . .

The Augsburg Confession is the primary statement of faith of the Lutheran Church. It was drawn up by Philip Melanchthon for presentation to the Diet of Augsburg of 1530. This diet was called by the Holy Roman Emperor Charles V so Lutherans and Roman Catholics could meet and iron out their differences. All parties involved agreed that Christianity was basically a commitment to certain essential points of doctrine. They expected that any reconciliation would be based upon a mutually acceptable statement of the essential teaching of the Christian faith. The Lutherans hoped that their Confession would effect a reconciliation.

Martin Luther recognized that the conciliatory Melanchthon, his friend, colleague, and right-hand man, was better suited than he to write a doctrinal statement for the purpose of reconciliation with Rome. Melanchthon used many of Luther's previous statements, however, in constructing the Confession, and so Luther was indirectly responsible for much of its content.

Melanchthon's original title for the Augsburg Confession was the "Augsburg Apology," because he designed it in answer to a list of over four hundred Lutheran "heresies" that the Catholics had presented to the emperor before the Diet of Augsburg convened. Melanchthon's strategy was to show that Lutherans were faithful to the teaching of the early church fathers, though they differed from medieval theology. Many versions of the Augsburg Confession exist, and there is scholarly debate over which version is authentic, though the differences between the versions are not major.

The Augsburg Confession is presented in two parts: (1) doctrines held in common by the Lutherans and the early church and (2) unacceptable corruptions that crept into the church during medieval times. These are presented with brevity, clarity, and force in a solidly evangelical form.

Part 1 of the Confession consists of twenty-one articles: The first seventeen present the fundamental points and the proper order of events in the gospel story as understood by the Lutherans. The remaining articles were added for clarification of an earlier point. Part 2 of the Confession addresses the corruptions or abuses that have crept into the church over the ages. No new theological ideas are introduced.

The Augsburg Confession is a brief document stressing only the essential points of the gospel. Though it is a noble statement, it failed in its purpose to unite Lutherans and Catholics. Still, it has served both as the basic document of Lutheranism up to the present and also as a model after which later Protestant statements of faith were patterned.

Institutes of the Christian Religion   1536
John Calvin

. . . .

Calvin was born in northwestern France in 1509, twenty-five years after the birth of Martin Luther. His actual name, Jean Cauvin, became "Calvin" years later when, as a scholar, he adopted the Latin form *Calvinus.* His birthplace, Noyon, was an old and important center of the Roman Catholic Church in northern Europe; a bishop resided there, and the economic, political, and social life of the city revolved largely around the cathedral. Calvin's father had become the bishop's secretary after serving the church in various other offices. As a result, young Calvin was closely tied to church affairs from his earliest childhood and was brought up with children of the aristocracy, a background that made him a much more refined reformer than the notoriously earthy Luther.

To enable Calvin to advance to a position of ecclesiastical importance, Calvin's father saw to it that his son received the best possible education. At age fourteen Calvin was enrolled at the University of Paris, the intellectual center of western Europe. There he eventually attended the Collège de Montaigu, the same institution Erasmus had attended some thirty years earlier.

Although Calvin began his education in theology, for several reasons his life took an unexpected turn. First, the new humanistic learning of the Renaissance was waging a successful battle against Scholasticism, the old Catholic theology of the late Middle Ages. Calvin encountered the new learning among the students and was powerfully attracted to it. Second, a strong movement for reform in the church, led by Jacques Lefèvre d'Étaples, had been flourishing in Paris not far from the university. Calvin became a close friend of some of Lefèvre's disciples. Third, Luther's writings and ideas had circulated in Paris for some time, causing a moderate stir; Calvin undoubtedly became familiar with them during his student years. Finally, Calvin's father had a falling-out with the church officials in Noyon, including the bishop. So in 1528, just as Calvin received the master of arts, his father sent word for him to leave theology and study law. Dutifully, Calvin migrated to Orléans, where France's best law faculty was located.

Calvin threw himself into his legal studies, winning acclaim for his mastery of the material and often teaching classes for absent professors. After about three years of study at Orléans, Bourges, and Paris, Calvin earned a doctorate in law and received his law license. Along the way he learned Greek and immersed himself in classical studies, which were of great interest to contemporary humanists. When his father's death in 1531 left Calvin free to choose the career he favored, he did not hesitate. Excited and challenged by his new studies, he moved to Paris to pursue a scholarly life. Had he not been converted to Protestantism, he would undoubtedly have lived out his days in Paris as a leading Renaissance scholar.

Little is known about Calvin's conversion except that it occurred between 1532 and early 1534, when his first religious work was published. When Nicholas Cop was elected rector of the University of Paris in 1533, his rectoral address strongly advocated reform along Lutheran lines. Whether Calvin actually contributed to the address, as is often supposed, is impossible to prove. His association was close enough, however, that when the rector was accused of heresy, they both fled the city.

Calvin returned to Paris shortly afterward, but only briefly, spending the next three years traveling throughout France, Switzerland, and Italy. In the spring of 1534 he returned to Noyon to resign his ecclesiastical benefice (regular income that had been granted him by the church and had supported him during his studies). No longer able to draw on that stipend with a clear conscience, Calvin burned his bridges to Roman Catholicism with his resignation.

When French king Francis I decided that persecution was the solution to the Protestant problem, Calvin realized it was no longer safe to live anywhere in France. He moved to Basel, Switzerland, where he published the first edition of his *Institutes of the Christian Religion* in 1536. When Calvin learned that Francis I objected to Protestantism because he thought it rejected all civil authority, Calvin rushed the *Institutes* to press with a dedication and preface to the king, acknowledging the king's authority and laying out the articles of Reformed faith in clear fashion. The work, which underwent several revisions before its final exhaustive edition in 1559, was without question one of the most influential handbooks on theology ever written.

Traveling to Strassburg in 1536, Calvin stopped for the night in Geneva. With the help of its Swiss neighbors, Geneva had recently declared its allegiance to Protestantism and its political independence from the Holy Roman Empire. When the city leaders learned of Calvin's presence in the city, they asked him to help lead the Genevan church. Calvin initially declined, explaining that he desired only to find a quiet refuge for study. But continued pressure eventually convinced Calvin to accept the task. The rest of his life was given mostly to the work of reform in Geneva.

Calvin immediately set to work reorganizing the church and

its worship. Calvin instituted various changes in the observance of the Lord's Supper and established a church board (the Genevan Consistory) to insure that all those participating in the Lord's Supper truly belonged to the "body of Christ." Calvin also introduced congregational singing into the church service.

After a couple of years in Geneva, however, Calvin created several influential enemies. Before Calvin's arrival in 1536, the city of Geneva was one of the most infamously immoral cities in Europe. Calvin's strict imposition of church discipline angered many of the citizens there, and he was eventually banished from the city.

Calvin spent the following three years (1538–1541) in Strassbourg, enjoying his long-sought period of peaceful study. There he associated closely with Martin Bucer, whose ideas, particularly on predestination, the Lord's Supper, and church organization, markedly influenced Calvin's own. In Strassbourg, Calvin also pastored a congregation of Protestant refugees from France, organizing its church government after what he believed to be the New Testament pattern and compiling a liturgy and popular psalmbook. He also participated as a representative of Strassbourg in the religious colloquies at Worms and Regensberg between Roman Catholics and Protestants.

In the meantime, the Roman Catholic Church, mindful of Calvin's expulsion from Geneva, judged that with some diplomatic care the city might be persuaded to return to Catholicism. Early in 1539 the city council received a letter urging such a move. The council was at a loss to find anyone in Geneva sufficiently competent to respond to the letter, so they forwarded it to Calvin in Strassbourg. His reply to the Roman Catholic Church stands as a brilliant explanation and justification of the Protestant Reformation.

Through a remarkable series of coincidences, the four principal Genevan leaders who had secured Calvin's exile were disgraced—all in unrelated incidents—and in 1541 the city asked Calvin to return. The prospect horrified Calvin, who regarded Geneva as "that cross on which I had to perish daily a thousand times over." Nevertheless, he reluctantly returned. The city council, now much more attentive to Calvin's proposals, approved his reforms with few emendations. Though constantly embroiled in controversy and bitterly opposed by strong political factions, Calvin pursued his tasks of pastoring and reform for many years in Geneva.

In addition to traditional areas of Christian works, such as arranging for the care of the elderly and the poor, many of Calvin's reforms reached into new areas: foreign affairs, law, economics, trade, and public policy. Calvin exemplified his own emphasis that in a Christian commonwealth every aspect of culture must be brought under Christ's lordship and treated as an area of Christian stewardship. Calvin worked on the recodification of Geneva's constitution and law, lessening the severity of many of the city's statutes and making them more humane. In addition, he helped negotiate treaties, encouraged the city's prosperous trade in cloth and velvet, and even proposed sanitary regulations and a sewage system. Calvin remained in Geneva, continuing his reforms until his death in 1564.

Calvin's reputation and esteem always seemed greatest among the population of Protestant refugees who flocked to the city, making Geneva the uncontested center of the Protestant movement. Missionaries fanned out from Geneva to the surrounding countries. The Reformed Church thus became the only Protestant group with a universal program.

In the past some have said that the sovereignty of God was Calvin's central teaching. Today many Calvin scholars argue that he made no attempt to reduce the biblical message to any one central idea but rather appreciated and retained the biblical teachings in their complexity. Many insist that Calvin affirmed both human responsibility and God's sovereign control.

Calvin's system does possess unity. Behind everything that he wrote is the idea suggested earlier by Augustine of Hippo: that God created human beings for fellowship with himself. Lacking that fellowship, they are miserable and disoriented. Thus, Calvin began his *Institutes* by stressing that all wisdom comes from a knowledge of God and of ourselves. This relationship between God and humanity was so basic for Calvin that he argued that in coming to know God, people learn about themselves, and vice versa.

In addition to theology, two areas in which Calvin made major contributions were education and church government. He encouraged the development of universal education. Calvin was convinced that, for every person to be adequately equipped to "rightly divide" God's Word, he or she had to be educated in languages and the humanities. To this end he founded an academy for Geneva's children, believing that all education must be fundamentally religious. The city's university grew out of the academy, offering an education comparable to the finest schools in Europe. Some have called the University of Geneva Calvin's "crowning achievement."

Calvin's ideas on church government, which have had a powerful effect on political theory in the West, are regarded by other scholars as his greatest contribution. The representative form of government he developed was organized so that basic decisions were made at the local level and monitored through a system of ascending representative bodies, culminating in a national general assembly with final authority. At each level power was shared with the laity, not controlled exclusively by the clergy or administrative officials. In emergencies the local church could function without meetings of the upper-level bodies. The organization of the Calvinist church helped it to survive and even flourish under adverse conditions. It experienced severe persecution in Holland, France, England, Scotland, Hungary, and elsewhere.

Calvin regarded himself primarily as a pastor and a theologian. Spending almost all of his productive years as a refugee and a foreigner in the Genevan republic, he was accorded citizenship only five years before his death, and then only after he appeared to be dying. Because his opinions were highly regarded, his political views were influential, but he never held political office. His cultural impact was not that of an autocrat but of a persuasive thinker who sought to apply biblical principles to every area of life.

Calvin was never much of a popular hero. Lacking the charm of Luther's blustering Germanic confidence and humor, Calvin held an intensely serious view of life. Sensing a divine call to the work of God's kingdom, he approached his task with great zeal and expected the same of others. Few lighthearted moments or intimate glimpses of Calvin were recorded. Humility and self-denial were his principal Christian virtues. He lived modestly, had few possessions, lived in borrowed quarters, and stubbornly refused salary increases.

Calvin's *Institutes of the Christian Religion* is regarded by many as one of the world's most influential works. The theological system laid out in this work gave birth to a distinctive "Reformed" theology, often referred to as "Calvinism." Reformed theology permeated many of the Protestant denominations that would later arise from the Reformation, and it even influenced much of Western political theory.

Institutes of the Christian Religion was first published in 1536. The initial edition of the *Institutes* was a long catechism or summary of the basic doctrines and principles essential to Protestantism. Additional material attacked false sacraments and presented Calvin's ideas for church organization. Calvin enlarged and expanded the work until, in 1559, the definitive Latin version of the *Institutes* was published. In its final form the *Institutes* was a comprehensive manual of dogmatic theology.

The 1536 edition of *Institutes of the Christian Religion* consists of a preface and six chapters. The preface is a dedicatory letter to the French king Francis I, defending the legitimacy of the Protestant faith.

Chapter 1 discusses the purposes of the law in the Bible. Here Calvin discusses each of the Ten Commandments and contrasts righteousness by faith with righteousness by works.

Chapter 2 addresses the significance of faith. It discusses the nature of faith and the Trinity and examines the tenets established by the Nicene Creed. The chapter concludes with a discussion of the relationship of faith, hope, and love in the life of the believer.

Prayer is the dominant topic of the third chapter, which contrasts Roman Catholic worship with evangelical worship. Congregational singing and the use of Latin are also discussed in this chapter.

The four sections of the fourth chapter examine the sacraments. The first section surveys questions about the sacraments in general; section 2 addresses the topic of baptism; section 3 discusses the Lord's Supper; and the fourth section details the proper administration of these sacraments. Calvin's basis for discerning true versus false sacramental theology is scriptural precedent, as opposed to human convention.

In chapter 5 Calvin targets five Roman Catholic sacramental teachings and practices that he believed to be false. He briefly discusses confirmation, extreme unction, and marriage. Concerning the sacrament of penance, Calvin contrasts scriptural repentance and forgiveness with Roman Catholic practices of repentance, confession, absolution, indulgences, treasury of merits, satisfaction for sins, and purgatory. Against the sacrament of ecclesiastical orders, Calvin introduces a scriptural doctrine of ministry. This fifth chapter forms Calvin's refutation of medieval church order.

Chapter 6 appears to be a conclusion to the dedicatory letter to Francis I, which prefaces the *Institutes.* This conclusion consists of three parts. The first is an essay on Christian freedom, meaning freedom from religious law, freedom of conscience, and freedom in other matters, such as diet and celibacy. The second part addresses ecclesiastical power. Church laws may be necessary for governing, but they are not necessary for salvation, and concerning them the conscience is free. The final part discusses the role of civil government. Magistrates provide for common safety and peace. Punishment with equity should be the goal of civil law. Such magistrates and laws exist for the people who are to respond in obedience. Calvin closes the *Institutes of the Christian Religion* with a quote from Acts 5:29 (KJV): "We ought to obey God rather than men," reminding readers that there is ultimately one King of kings.

King James (Authorized) Version of the Holy Bible 1611

After James VI of Scotland became the king of England (and was renamed James I), he invited several clergymen from Puritan and Anglican factions to meet together with the hope that differences could be reconciled. Though the meeting failed to reconcile the two parties, it did turn out to be profitable. During the meeting John Reynolds, a Puritan leader and president of Corpus Christi College, Oxford, asked the king to authorize a new, more accurate translation of the Bible into English. James liked this idea, especially since he opposed the seemingly seditious notes that accompanied the Geneva Bible.

The king initiated the work and took an active part in planning the new translation. He suggested that university professors work on the translation to assure the best scholarship, and he strongly urged that they not have any marginal notes besides those pertaining to literal renderings from the Hebrew and Greek. The absence of interpretive notes would help the translation to be accepted by all the churches in England.

More than fifty scholars, who were trained in Hebrew and Greek, began the work in 1607. The translation went through several committees before it was finalized. The scholars were instructed to follow the already existing Bishops' Bible as the basic version, as long as it adhered to the original text. They were also instructed to consult the translations of Tyndale, Matthew, and Coverdale, as well as the Great Bible and the Geneva Bible when they appeared to contain more accurate renderings of the original languages. This dependence on other versions is expressed in the preface to the King James Version: "Truly, good Christian reader, we never thought from the beginning that we should need to make a new translation, nor yet to make of a bad one a good one . . . but to make a good one better, or out of many good ones one principal good one."

The King James Version captured the best of all the preceding English translations and far exceeded all of them. Indeed, the King James Version, known in England as the Authorized Version because it was authorized by the king, has become an enduring monument of English prose because of its graceful style, majestic language, and poetic rhythms. No other book has had such a tremendous influence on English literature.

The King James Version became the most popular English translation in the seventeenth, eighteenth, and nineteenth centuries. It became the standard English Bible for hundreds of years, and it has even influenced the English language itself. This version has been revised again and again throughout the centuries in the following versions: the English Revised Version (1884), the American Standard Version (1901), the Revised Standard Version (1952), and the New King James Version (1982). But not one of these revisions has outstripped the King James Version's popularity, which, despite its lofty Elizabethan English, is still enjoyed by millions today.

Westminster Confession 1648

The Westminster Confession of Faith was produced at the Westminster Assembly and adopted by the English Parliament in 1648. The Assembly was originally commissioned by Parliament to revise the Thirty-nine Articles of the Church of England; but when the Solemn League and Covenant between England and Scotland appeared in 1643, the Assembly was recommissioned to draw up a confession of faith for the entire kingdom.

The Westminster proceedings were too slow for the Church of Scotland General Assembly, which tried unsuccessfully to expedite matters in 1645. Pressure from the House of Commons finally effected the completion of the Confession in 1646. The House of Commons was not satisfied with this version, however, and so several "proof texts" were added to the third limited edition in 1647.

When copies of the third edition reached the Church of Scotland General Assembly late in 1647, Robert Baillie, one of the Scottish commissioners at Westminster, told his fellow churchmen that the Confession was perfected with far greater unanimity than anyone living could have hoped for. The General Assembly approved it and declared it to be standard for the church. The Scottish Parliament approved it two years later.

English House of Commons began debate over the Confession in May of 1647 and continued for ten months until its adoption. Its formal title was: Articles of Christian religion approved and passed by both Houses of Parliament, after advice had with the Assembly of Divines, by authority of Parliament sitting at Westminster. The welcome in England for the Westminster Confession of Faith was not as enthusiastic as it was in Scotland, and the Westminster Confession never became the creed of England. It was first published for general circulation in June 1648.

The Westminster Confession is remarkable for its clarity and compactness, and for reflecting what has been called "a theological consensus of international Calvinism." It is divided into thirty-three chapters, which cover seven aspects of divine revelation. These are Scripture, God, humanity, Christ, salvation, the church, and last things. The order of the material is different from the Thirty-nine Articles of Anglicanism and other Scottish confessions. The Confession was strongly influenced by the Irish Articles drawn up by Archbishop James Ussher and ratified by the Protestant Church in Ireland in 1615.

The Westminster Confession was officially abandoned by Anglicanism with the Restoration in 1660, but it helped mold the character of English and American Presbyterianism, and it made some impact also in Baptist and Congregationalist circles. Its lasting mark has been in Scotland, where rigid adherence to the Westminster Confession is still an essential feature of smaller Presbyterian groups. Even the national Church of Scotland still holds as a subordinate standard the Westminster Confession of Faith. There the Confession is modified by certain Declaratory Acts, and subscription to it is required before ministers are ordained.

Paradise Lost   1667
John Milton

. . . .

John Milton was born in London in 1608. His father, a scrivener and an accomplished musician, afforded Milton an extraordinary education, including seven years at Christ's College, Cambridge, six years of postgraduate private study, and fifteen months of travel, primarily in Italy.

Milton enjoyed languages. He especially loved Latin and Italian and wrote poems in both languages. He read Homer, Plato, and the New Testament writers from the original Greek; his knowledge of Hebrew and Aramaic enabled him to read the Old Testament and the Jewish commentators like a scholar. In addition to French and Spanish, he probably also read Anglo-Saxon. Milton even agreed to teach someone Greek in return for lessons in an American Indian language. Hardly a single area of study and culture escaped Milton's attention, and the keystone of all his learning was the Bible.

With the outbreak of the English Civil War in 1642, Milton allied himself with the Parliamentary Party. When Cromwell came into power, Milton was sought out by Parliament to serve as Latin secretary to the council of state and as chief apologist for the government.

In 1643 Milton married Mary Powell, the daughter of a prominent Royalist. A few months after the wedding, Mary returned to the home of her parents. She remained separated from Milton for three years but eventually returned and bore her first child, a daughter. In time she gave birth to three other children but died giving birth to the last one. The third child, a son whom they named John, died one month after his mother.

At the age of forty-seven Milton married Katherine Woodcock, who bore a daughter a year later. Within a few months both the mother and daughter died.

Cromwell's death in 1658 resulted in the loss of Milton's secretaryship. In 1660, shortly before Charles II returned from France to restore the monarchy, Milton published *A Free and Easy Way to Establish a Free Commonwealth.* Immediately following the Restoration, Milton faced great danger. He was forced to go into hiding until influential friends interceded on his behalf. From the early 1660s until his death in 1674, Milton lived a quiet life, arranged in part by his third wife, Elizabeth Minsul.

Milton's writings may be roughly divided into three periods.

He produced his first group of poems and prose before the outbreak of the English Civil War in 1642. By the age of twenty-four he had written three excellent poems: "On the Meaning of Christ's Nativity," "L'Allegro," and "Il Penseroso." During the next six years he wrote several other poems, including "Comus" and "Lycidas."

The second period of Milton's writings coincides roughly with the outbreak of the English Civil War. He wrote scholarly and polemical essays on religious, social, educational, and domestic responsibility.

During the period from 1660 until the end of his life, Milton produced his greatest works. The epic *Paradise Lost* (1667) poetically recounts the biblical story of humanity's creation and fall. This tragedy was followed by the triumphant *Paradise Regained* (1671), which recalls the temptation of Jesus, who, unlike Adam, would not fall. *Samson Agonistes* (1671), portrays Samson's trials and triumph in the form of Greek tragedy.

John Milton began writing his masterwork, *Paradise Lost,* sometime between 1655 and 1658 and finished it by 1667. This epic poem retells the biblical story of creation, of the fall of Satan, and of the fall of humanity. Milton added detail and drama to the biblical account through poetic imagery and rhythm, lending powerful originality to the familiar story. The Genesis drama is embellished by Milton's imagination and by imagery drawn from other literature.

The subject of Milton's grand poem is made clear in the opening verses: "Of man's first disobedience, and the fruit/ Of that forbidden tree whose mortal taste/ Brought death into the world, and all our woe,/With loss of Eden, till one greater Man/Restore us, and regain the blissful seat."

Milton did not follow the biblical sequence of events in his account. Instead he used flashbacks and flash-forwards to rearrange the chronology of the creation story, which is usually presented as (1) the war in heaven; (2) the creation of the universe; (3) Adam and Eve in Paradise; (4) the temptation and fall of humankind; and (5) the aftermath of the Fall, which is human history.

The poem is composed of twelve books. In books one and two Satan's army is defeated. After debating with the fallen angels, Satan decides to fly to the world and pervert humanity. A council in heaven is recounted in book three. God observes Satan's journey to earth and tells his Son that Satan will succeed in corrupting Adam and Eve. Christ offers to become mortal and to pay "death for death" in order that neither man nor justice dies eternally.

Book four describes Adam and Eve in Eden and includes a flashback to Eve's creation. In book five the angel Raphael tells Adam the story of the war in heaven, and book six describes the creation of the universe. God sent Raphael to tell Adam of Satan's rebellion and of his plot against humanity. In this way God gave Adam and Eve the freedom to choose good over evil. The seventh book of *Paradise Lost* gives Raphael's rich description of the world created by God and climaxes with a chorus of thanksgiving.

The flashback of book eight relates Adam and Eve's own story of their creation and marriage. Book nine portrays Adam on the morning of the temptation, pleading with Eve not to leave his side. Eve believes she is strong enough to resist evil. Her pride and overconfidence allow Satan, in the guise of the serpent, to deceive her. The consequence of the Fall on earth and in hell is described in book ten. Finally, Michael the archangel leads Adam and Eve out of the Garden. He reveals to them the future course of biblical history, including the good news that there will be a Savior to redeem humankind (books eleven and twelve).

Paradise Lost is considered by many to be the clearest, most moving poetry in the English language. A poem by Samuel Barrow, included in the 1674 edition of Milton's epic work, aptly asks, "He who reads *Paradise Lost,* what does he read but everything? All things and the origin of all things."

Pia Desideria (Pious Desires)   1675
Philipp Jakob Spener
. . . .

Philipp Jakob Spener was born in the Alsatian village of Rappoltstein at the height of the Thirty Years' War (1635). The spiritual climate of Germany at this time could accurately be described as dry, formal—a religion of the disciplined mind. Ministers were trained in the propositions of orthodox Lutheranism and the art of philosophical debate. The Calvinists and the Roman Catholic Church were both considered enemies of the true faith. Lutheranism in Spener's day had degenerated to a religion of the mind and had little relevance for the common layperson.

Spener was raised in a highly protective and deeply religious atmosphere. As a boy he was an avid reader, and his favorite book next to the Bible was *True Christianity* by Johann Arndt. This book did much to shape Spener's thought, asserting the limited value of orthodox doctrine and the importance of pious living and active love. In 1651 Spener became a student of theology at Strassburg, studying under the strict Lutheran J. K. Dannhauer. He then spent a number of years studying at Basel, Geneva, Stuttgart, and Tübingen. In Geneva, Spener came into contact with Reformed theology and the doctrines of repentance and regeneration. All these experiences were formative to Spener's life and thought.

In 1663 Spener became a free preacher at Strassburg, at which time he received his doctor of theology degree (1664). During this time he also served as pastor and senior of the ministerium in Frankfurt, where he eventually emerged as the leader of the

Pietist movement in Germany. Spener was appointed court chaplain at Dresden in 1686, but a poor relationship with the ruling Saxon family made his stay there short-lived. In 1691 he accepted an invitation to the pastorate of Saint Nicholas Church in Berlin.

While at Frankfurt, Spener did much to reform the standard religious instruction of his day. He advocated a contextual approach to biblical preaching, restored the confirmation service, set aside days of fasting and prayer, and asserted the need for conversion and holy living. He is probably best known for setting up what he called *collegia pietatis*—small groups of pastors and laymen that met together for Bible study and prayer. He saw these as small churches within the church and believed them to be necessary for strengthening pastors and laity alike. Spener modeled his small groups upon similar bodies among the Reformed churches, and with time these became an important feature in much of German Lutheranism.

Little of Spener's teaching was original, but it was timely and forcefully argued. His emphasis upon the new birth and holy living effectively undermined the position of scholastic Lutheran orthodoxy, doing much to revitalize the German Lutheran Church of his day. He called the church to a life of piety, to a faith that not only used the mind but touched the heart and inspired the hands as well.

Spener's best-known writing, *Pia Desideria* (Pious Desires), was originally written in 1675 to preface an edition of Johann Arndt's book *True Christianity*. It was later issued separately under the title *Pia Desideria or Heartfelt Desire for a God-pleasing Reform of the True Evangelical Church, Together with Several Simple Christian Proposals Looking toward This End.*

This tract outlined Spener's hopes and intentions for the reform of the Protestant church. It established the primary tenets of Pietism—Bible study, the priesthood of all believers, faith expressed not in knowledge but in acts of love toward others, and the avoidance of theological arguments. Spener believed the spiritual life of the believer was more important than "correct" doctrine and felt that preaching should call its hearers to more pious living rather than deeper philosophical thinking. Spener's approach brought a radical critique on the ministerial training of his day, while calling the laity to a pious and active faith.

Pia Desideria can be divided into three sections. First, Spener details the shortcomings of the political and clerical authorities of his day. He also points out weaknesses among the laity and the moral looseness of society in general. Next, drawing on the promises of the Bible and the example of the early church, Spener emphasizes the prospect for reform in the church.

Finally, six substantial strategies are offered for reform: (1) renewed study of the Scriptures; (2) greater participation from the laity; (3) practical application of the teachings of Christianity; (4) avoidance of antagonistic scholastic disputes; (5) emphasis upon piety in the training of clergy; and (6) emphasis upon spiritual development in preaching.

The Pilgrim's Progress   1678
John Bunyan

Born at Elstow, Bedfordshire, in 1628, John Bunyan went either to the newly founded grammar school at Bedford or to the more humble one at Elstow. He married when he was twenty-one. After reading two religious books brought home by his wife, Bunyan experienced an awakened sense of religion and began to change many of his habits. Despite these outward changes, however, Bunyan began to realize his need for something deeper. One day he overheard a conversation about spiritual matters while pursuing his craft as a tinker. He was completely unfamiliar with the "inner experience" of which the people spoke, and this conversation eventually led to his conversion.

In 1653 Bunyan settled in Bedford, joining an independent congregation there. When he began preaching in 1657, news that the once blaspheming tinker had turned preacher drew crowds from far away to hear him.

In 1656 Bunyan had published his first written work, a pamphlet against the Quakers called *Some Gospel Truths Opened*. This was answered by Edward Burroughs, an ardent Quaker, and Bunyan replied the following year with *A Vindication of Some Gospel Truths Opened*. His third work was a book about the parable of the rich man and Lazarus called *Sighs from Hell, or the Groans of a Damned Soul* (1658).

In 1660 persecution against Nonconformists was revived: Meeting houses were closed; all persons were required to attend their parish church; and it was illegal to conduct worship services except in accordance with Anglican ritual. Bunyan continued to preach in barns, in private homes, under trees, or in churches if invited. He was arrested in November 1660 on his way to conduct a religious service about twelve miles from Bedford.

The circumstances of Bunyan's imprisonment were less severe than some have maintained. There was no prohibition on visitors, and the regular appearance of his publications increased his reputation. He also wrote *Grace Abounding to the Chief of Sinners, Christian Behavior,* and *The Holy City* during this time. In the early days of his imprisonment, he attended Bedford Church, but after October 1661 his name was not again on the attendance record until October 1668; evidently his confinement became stricter. After 1668 he appears to have been paroled, although his formal pardon did not come until 1672.

Bunyan published his famous allegory *The Pilgrim's Progress* in 1678. Early in the Christian tradition, pilgrimage had come to represent the journey through life or the progress of human life to a state of blessedness. In *The Pilgrim's Progress* the pilgrim is a human soul in quest of peace with God.

The Pilgrim's Progress was followed by two more allegorical books, *The Life and Death of Mr. Badman* (1680) and *The Holy War* (1682). In 1684 Bunyan published a *Second Part to the Pilgrim's Progress,* a sequel in which the pilgrim's wife and children, accompanied by Mercy, follow the same route and enter the Celestial City.

Bunyan authored many lesser-known books, but *The Pilgrim's Progress* has been translated into hundreds of languages and dialects. His archetypal figures—the pilgrim, the burden, the monsters, the road with its sloughs and bypaths, the true and false guides, the resting places, and the final goal of the heavenly city—seem to connect with people of all ages in all countries.

On one of his preaching journeys to London in August 1688, Bunyan went out of his way to Reading to help settle a quarrel between a father and son. After riding through heavy rain, he arrived at the home of a London friend. He preached the following Sunday, but in a few days he developed a violent fever and died. He was buried in Bunhill Fields, London.

The complete title of John Bunyan's most popular work is *The Pilgrim's Progress From This World To That Which Is To Come, Delivered Under The Similitude Of A Dream Wherein Is Discovered The Manner Of His Setting Out, His Dangerous Journey, And Safe Arrival At The Desired Country.* This allegory of the Christian life and Puritan ideals was published in two parts. Part 1 was composed during Bunyan's twelve-year imprisonment. It describes the journey of Christian from the City of Destruction to the Celestial City. Part 2, published several years later, recounts a gentler version of the same journey: Christian's wife, Christiana, and their children undertake the journey to the

Celestial City as well. Both parts draw from Bunyan's earlier work, *Grace Abounding to the Chief of Sinners.*

The Pilgrim's Progress, part 1, has one main character, Christian, who is the pilgrim throughout the story. He is a poor, ragged man who flees from the wicked City of Destruction and sets out on a pilgrimage to find the Celestial City. In describing this journey, Bunyan has translated many of his own personal experiences into a parable filled with vividly recognizable characters and locations.

As Christian flees the City of Destruction, he falls into the Slough of Despond, a swamp of pilgrims' doubts and fears. Near the Village of Morality, Christian meets Mr. Worldly Wiseman, who has come to terms with the world on a moral level. The friendly Mr. Wiseman nearly convinces Christian to settle in the Village of Morality, but he is berated by Evangelist, who urges him on his way to the Wicket Gate. There the gatekeeper, Good-will, opens the gate, and Christian enters the straight and narrow Holy Way. But Good-will cannot relieve Christian of the heavy sack of sins he has been carrying so long.

Christian's first stop along the Holy Way is the large house of Interpreter, who symbolizes the Holy Spirit. Interpreter shows Christian a number of "excellent things" about the Christian life. After this, Christian comes to the cross and an open grave beneath it. There the burden on Christian's back slips and rolls into the grave. Three Shining Ones tell him that his sins are forgiven, and then they give him bright new clothes and a rolled parchment to read for teaching and comfort along the way. Continuing on, Christian has to crawl inch by inch up Difficulty Hill. His companions, Formalist and Hypocrisy, are no help. Halfway up he falls asleep from exhaustion. In his rush to the top, Christian leaves behind the parchment, and he must backtrack down the hill to retrieve it. Eventually, he comes to the Palace Beautiful, where four virgins, Discretion, Prudence, Piety, and Charity give him lodging and in the morning send him away with weapons and armor for his dangerous journey.

Christian is attacked by the monster Apollyon in the Valley of Humiliation. By means of All-prayer, Christian passes near the mouth of Hell in the desertlike Valley of the Shadow of Death. At the end of the Valley, he joyfully finds Faithful, his neighbor from the City of Destruction. Together they must pass through the town of Vanity Fair, a sort of year-round flea market. The two pilgrims are arrested because they will only buy the Truth. Faithful is burned at the stake, but Christian escapes.

Christian soon comes to By-path Meadow, where a giant named Despair locks him in Doubting Castle. Christian finds the Key of Promise and escapes, and then he moves on to the Delectable Mountains and the Country of Beulah. Christian's faith is again tested when he must cross the swift dark river of death. But on the far side he enters the Celestial City at the top of Mighty Hill, where people walk on streets of gold and play golden harps.

The Pilgrim's Progress brought instantaneous recognition and success to John Bunyan. It was popular among people of every class in England and has gone through many hundreds of editions. Historically, it is the most widely read Christian book next to the Bible. As literature, *The Pilgrim's Progress* has been the subject of commentaries and criticism from the time of its publication until today. It is considered by many to be the last great expression of Christian folk tradition.

The Practice of the Presence of God   c. 1693
Brother Lawrence

Born in Lorraine, France, near the beginning of the seventeenth century, Brother Lawrence was originally named Nicholas Herman. After a relatively obscure childhood, Lawrence entered the army during the Thirty Years' War, remaining a soldier for eighteen years. Later he served in Paris as an assistant to the treasurer of France. While there, Lawrence became enamored with the life of the severe order of Discalced Carmelites. Around 1651 he made his profession there and continued in it for the remainder of his life. He never sought advancement beyond the humble status of lay brother, serving his community as a cook for thirty years. He was eventually released from his duties because of blindness, and he died a few years later.

Brother Lawrence left no major writings, except for a few spiritual notes and letters. Within a short time after his death, however, his simple writings were assembled and published in 1691. Two years later a shorter version was published, some of which has been translated, edited, and published as *The Practice of the Presence of God.* Lawrence's quasi-mystical spirituality held considerable appeal for many believers, both from the Roman Catholic Church and from various Protestant denominations.

Brother Lawrence's book, *The Practice of the Presence of God,* was compiled from his letters, from personal interviews, and from a short manuscript entitled *Maxims,* which was found among Brother Lawrence's possessions after his death. It is a collection of Lawrence's reflections on everything from prayer to daily work.

Lawrence actually wrote his first letter on the condition that it be shown to no one else. Throughout his letters, Lawrence reveals his desire for deep intimacy with God.

The personal interviews with Brother Lawrence discuss his way to "establish ourselves in a sense of God's presence." This is done "by continually conversing with Him. [It is] a shameful thing to quit His conversation to think of trifles and fooleries." By the time of these conversations, Lawrence had been working in the monastery kitchen for fifteen years. For him, God was present in every situation of life, and believers should strive to perform every action with this understanding.

Brother Lawrence tried to conduct his life by the love of God, performing every deed by this single motivation. Lawrence was not impressed with good works by themselves; he was more concerned that good works reflect the love of God in the heart of the one performing them.

In the late seventeenth century it was radical to proclaim, as Brother Lawrence did, "To be with God there is no need to be continually in church. Of our heart we may make an oratory, wherein to retire from time to time and with Him hold meek, humble, loving converse." For Brother Lawrence, God could be encountered anywhere, although it is important to understand that Lawrence was not denying the need for believers to attend church. He was simply trying to remove the barriers between sacred and secular life. Lawrence insisted that "the time of action is not different from that of prayer. I enjoy God with as great tranquility in the hurry of my kitchen, where frequently many people call upon me at the same time for different things, as if I was on my knees at the holy sacrament."

The Eighteenth and Nineteenth Centuries

A Serious Call to a Devout and Holy Life 1728
William Law
. . . .

William Law was born at King's Cliffe, Northamptonshire, to a
family of substantial means. He attended Emmanuel College,
Cambridge, where he became a fellow. In 1712, a year after his
ordination, he earned a master of arts degree, following intensive
study in the classics and philosophy. It was probably at this time
that he began to read the early English mystics and became
acquainted with classical devotional writers, such as Saint
Francis de Sales and Thomas à Kempis.

When the Hanoverian king George I came to the throne, Law
refused to take an oath of allegiance. In consequence he forfeited
his fellowship at the university and permanently lost the right to
preach in the Church of England.

Little is known of Law's actions after that disappointment, but
it is believed that he went to London. In 1723 Law became affili-
ated with the Gibbon family in Putney, where he served as tutor
and chaplain to the household. After Edward Gibbon died, the
household broke up in 1737, and Law returned to his native
King's Cliffe, where he remained for the rest of his life. In his

later years, Law, together with Sarah Hutchinson and Hester Gibbon, founded several almshouses and a school.

Law wrote a number of works throughout his lifetime. His first significant writing was *Three Letters to the Bishop of Bangor* (1717), an effective apologetic for orthodox Christianity. In his *Practical Treatise Upon Christian Perfection* (1726), he laid down rules for achieving a life of piety. Law's most notable work, *A Serious Call to a Devout and Holy Life,* was published in 1728. Though Law's writings lack an emphasis upon Christ's redemptive ministry, their insight into devotional life influenced such evangelists as George Whitefield and John Wesley.

William Law wrote *A Serious Call to a Devout and Holy Life* while still in his early thirties. In it he raised a formidable challenge to his unbelieving age and profoundly influenced many minds of his time. Samuel Johnson commented on his encounter with *A Serious Call to a Devout and Holy Life* while a student at Oxford. He said, "I expected to find it a dull book . . . but I found Law quite an overmatch for me." Law presented his arguments in a way that made it credible to believe in Christianity without losing intellectual integrity.

The basic premise throughout *A Serious Call* assumes that the devout person is centered in God. He said that a devout life is "a better sacrifice to God than any forms of holy and heavenly prayers." Law believed that devotion to God is humanity's highest attainment and that true freedom is expressed in the believer's devotion to the redeemer-God. This devotion is a sign of true genius, "a soul in its highest state of knowledge."

The first half of the book sets a standard for honoring God in outward affairs. The second half is a guide to prayer and the ordering of the inner life. Law gives specific instructions for prayer and for the right use of money. For Law, every area of life should reflect the believer's devotion to God.

A Treatise Concerning Religious Affections 1746
Jonathan Edwards
. . . .

Born in 1703 at East Windsor, Connecticut, Jonathan Edwards
received his early education from his father, a Congregational
minister. He entered Yale College at the age of thirteen and grad-
uated in 1720. He remained at the college until August of 1722
to study for the ministry. After his studies he became a minister
of a Scottish Presbyterian church in New York. In 1723 he
returned to Yale, passed the examination for a master of arts degree, and assumed the office of tutor in May of 1724. He
resigned two years later because of illness. In 1726 he accepted a
call to become the colleague of his aging grandfather, the Rever-
end Solomon Stoddard, at Northampton, Massachusetts. He married Sarah Pierrepont the following year and assumed full
ministerial duties when Stoddard died in 1729.

Under the influence of Edwards's preaching, Northampton
and neighboring parishes experienced a powerful spiritual awakening in 1734 and 1735. His reputation as a preacher and an
advocate of experiential religion grew quickly. Beginning in
1739, again under the influence of Edwards's preaching, another
more extensive religious revival occurred, known as the Great
Awakening. During this time Edwards made the acquaintance of
George Whitefield, who was instrumental in promoting Edwards
abroad. The most famous sermon preached during the Great
Awakening, and likely the most famous sermon in all of American history, was Edwards's "Sinners in the Hands of an Angry
God," delivered in Enfield in 1741.

Controversy arose between Edwards and his congregation
when he tried to restrict Communion to those who could give sat-
isfactory evidence of conversion. In 1750 he was dismissed from
his charge at Northampton, and the following year he resettled in
Stockbridge, Massachusetts, where he led the small Stockbridge

church and served as teacher and missionary to the Housatonnoc Indians, who resided in the vicinity. In 1758 he reluctantly assumed duties as president of the College of New Jersey (later Princeton University), but he died a month later of a smallpox inoculation.

Regarded as the leading theologian of his day and one of the greatest thinkers America has yet produced, Edwards's importance rests primarily upon his contributions in the areas of practical and theoretical religion and his championing of evangelical Calvinism. Two early sermons laid the groundwork. "God Glorified in Man's Dependence," delivered in Boston in 1731 and published a month later, attacked the liberal notions of sin and salvation. In true Calvinist style, Edwards insisted that sin was inherent antagonism against God and that salvation meant a radical change of heart that was totally dependent upon the absolute sovereignty of God. In a second sermon, "A Divine and Supernatural Light," preached in 1733 and later published in 1734, Edwards described the true nature of religious experience. He explained that salvation does not involve simply a rational understanding of God and biblical truth, but, rather, it is a supernatural work of God in the heart of the believer. True religion, Edwards insisted, is essentially a matter of the heart, not the mind. These two sermons set forth a theological platform from which Edwards never wavered.

During the first Great Awakening, Edwards wrote two influential works in defense of the revival. *The Distinguishing Marks of a Work of the Spirit of God,* published in 1741, defended the revival as authentic by distinguishing "true signs" of religious experience from "false signs." In 1743 this work was expanded and published as *Some Thoughts Concerning the Present Revival.* In addition to answering the critics of the revival, here Edwards also warned against the sometimes aberrant nature of religious experience in order to temper revival enthusiasts.

Edwards's most mature analysis of religious experience, *A Treatise Concerning Religious Affections,* was published in 1746, several years after the revival was spent. This work defines the nature of religious experience as a matter of the heart, stating that true religion is seated in the affections or inclinations. *Religious Affections* identifies and examines false signs of true religion and describes twelve marks that arise from a genuine religious conversion.

Edwards's most significant theological and philosophical works were produced after his move to Stockbridge in 1751. In *Freedom of the Will,* published in 1754, he defended the Calvinist position by arguing that, prior to an individual's choosing or willing, there is a more basic cause identified as motive. This carries significant implications for conversion. By God's regenerative act, a new motive or "sense of the heart" is implanted in the soul, directing the will to God. The unregenerate are devoid of this new "sense," which comes through a supernatural act of God. They are not motivated by love for God but are rather given to self-love. Edwards defends this view of human nature in *The Great Christian Doctrine of Original Sin,* published in 1758. The subject of these two monumental works, themselves a development of the subject treated in *Religious Affections,* is continued in the shorter but no less significant *The Nature of True Virtue,* published posthumously in 1765.

Edwards's entire life and ministry were devoted to understanding and promoting true religion. In his estimation, the pursuit of true religion is the "greatest and most fundamental" duty of the Christian.

In *A Treatise Concerning Religious Affections,* Jonathan Edwards insisted that the essence of all true religion lies in holy love. He observed that there were many powerful inward experiences of God during the Great Awakening, but outward expressions of grace in the lives of people were rare. In *Religious*

Affections Edwards tried to develop a reliable series of signs by which genuine religious affections (expressions of God's grace) could be distinguished from other more spurious feelings. Edwards had lost confidence in subjective forms of religious consciousness. He had learned that these could be forms of self-deception. Instead, he relied on publicly manifested Christian practice as the true test of religious experience.

The book is divided into three parts. The first defines the nature of religious experience, noting that true religion is primarily a matter of the heart and is seated in the affections. The second identifies and examines false signs of true religion. The third, which takes up nearly three quarters of the treatise, describes twelve marks that arise from a genuine religious conversion.

Edwards uses 1 Peter 1:8 as the starting point for his compelling argument: "Whom having not seen, ye love; in whom, though now ye see him not, yet believing, ye rejoice with joy unspeakable and full of glory" (KJV). From this verse he develops his view of true religion: It consists of the affections of love and joy in Christ. Love depends on the spiritual sight of faith, while joy is the fruit of that faith. From this text he eventually derives the doctrine: "True religion, in great part, consists of holy affections." Such affections are exercises of the believer's will. They seek to possess divine glory in pure love. To Edwards, pure love is both the source of all true religious affections and the chief affection itself.

The third and most substantial section of *Religious Affections* gives an exhaustive account of twelve signs of religious affections. Edwards emphasizes that these signs are not for discerning true or false affections in others, but rather they should be used to examine one's own self.

As Edwards discusses the first sign, he fleshes out the biblical meaning of *spiritual, supernatural,* and *divine.* These are the only influences that produce genuine affections. The second sign is that a person's love for God is not dependent on the belief that God loves him or has forgiven him. Third, if an affection springs from an individual's concern for his own welfare, it is false. Fourth, gracious affections are based on spiritual understanding; therefore, they involve the will and the heart rather than mental speculation or observation.

The fifth sign asserts that genuine affections are accompanied by an immediate certainty of the truth of religion. Sixth, true affection involves voluntary humiliation before God. Seventh, true affections include a change of nature that, although not instantaneous or complete, is known by its permanence.

Signs eight and nine insist that the believer should face the world with meekness and tenderness. The tenth sign evaluates the symmetry of God's workmanship in a believer, emphasizing balance in the believer's life. The eleventh sign is an increase in the believer's appetite for God rather than an increase in self-satisfaction.

Sign twelve is to Edwards "the chief of all the signs of grace": Holy affections are seen in the believer's daily practice. Jonathan Edwards said, "Men's deeds are better and more faithful interpreters of their minds than their words." For Edwards, a truly repentant believer must walk the walk as well as talk the talk.

Journal 1771
John Woolman

Born in Northampton, New Jersey, in 1720, Woolman was raised on a farm. His Quaker grandfather had been among the first settlers in west Jersey, just across the Delaware River from Pennsylvania, the center of Quaker settlement in America. As a young man, Woolman moved to Mount Holly, where he worked as a tailor. This trade would support him at various times throughout his life. He owned a tailor shop for a time, but his desire for a deeper spiritual life led him to simplify his life. Deeply pious, he became a recorded minister of the Society of Friends (1743) and for thirty-seven years served as chairman for the quarterly business meeting in Burlington County. He began to travel extensively—thirty-nine trips in twenty-five years—ministering to Quaker communities throughout the thirteen colonies. Woolman died of smallpox on a visit to Friends in England and was buried at York in 1772.

John Woolman's *Journal* reveals a man who desired to follow the "pure leading" of God undistorted by natural human self-interest. He was conspicuous, even among Quakers, for his intense mystical piety. Woolman's America was a world of economic growth and agricultural expansion. The need for labor brought slaves from Africa. The need for land resulted in war with the Indians. In this world of slavery, Indian abuse, and war, Woolman desired to bring reform. He was concerned that Friends not take part in the injustices that seemed to pervade Colonial America. He believed that most, if not all, of society's problems could be traced to the pervasive principle of selfish pragmatism. In remedy, he called his fellow Quakers to live according to the principle of selfless love.

Woolman preached and wrote against slavery during a time when the practice was little questioned, and his testimony caused Quakers of the Philadelphia yearly meeting to denounce the practice in 1776. As a result of his efforts, many Friends, even some in the southern colonies, chose to free their slaves. Woolman also preached and wrote against the abuse of Indians, the ill-treatment of the poor, and conscription and taxation to support the war effort. He was a prophetic voice to Colonial America, but his influence was only significantly felt among the small population of Friends. Yet a century after his death, his writings (*Some Considerations on the Keeping of Negroes* and his

Journal) made a significant impact upon the abolitionist movement in the nineteenth century. Woolman's call to deeper spiritual life, defense of the helpless, and selfless action speaks to Christians of all centuries.

John Woolman's *Journal* has become a classic among Quaker works. He began his *Journal* when he was thirty-six years old and continued it until his death. In 1771 the poet John Greenleaf Whittier published the *Journal* with an informative introduction. This edition went through a number of printings, and Woolman's *Journal* was eventually chosen for inclusion among the Harvard Classics.

John Woolman's *Journal* records his spiritual development as he worked and traveled among the Society of Friends. He notes the development of his sensitive conscience that compelled him to publicly express his convictions. His *Journal* contains stories of his religious growth, which began before he was seven years old.

Woolman's *Journal* reveals his sensitivity to those who are suffering. From animals to Indians to slaves, Woolman repeatedly expressed his concern for those who were abused and considered of little significance. Because Woolman was literate, unlike most Americans, he was often called upon to draw up legal documents. Once when he was compelled to write the bill of sale for a slave, Woolman became so uneasy in his conscience that he openly denounced slavery as he wrote the bill. Shortly afterward he began his lifelong crusade against slavery. Woolman is given credit for the abolition of slavery among the Society of Friends before the Revolution.

Woolman's *Journal* also records how he refused to use many things because of their connection with slavery. He refused to eat sugar or wear dyed cloth. When crossing to England, Woolman's conscience would not allow him to take space in the cabin of the ship. Through Woolman's *Journal,* readers can peer inside a heart of deep conviction and piety.

Journal   c. 1791
John Wesley
. . . .

Born in Epworth, England, in 1703, John Wesley was the fifteenth child and second surviving son of Susanna and Samuel Wesley. Samuel was a former Nonconformist and rector at Epworth. He and his wife raised their children in an atmosphere of piety and Puritan discipline. John was educated at the Charterhouse School, London, and Christ Church, Oxford. He was elected fellow of Lincoln College, Oxford, in 1726, and received the master of arts in 1727. Wesley's short tenure as assistant to his father at Wroote (1727–1729) was his only experience in a parish.

A letter from the rector of Lincoln brought Wesley back to his duties at Oxford, where he joined his brother Charles, George Whitefield, and others in a venture that was to be the cradle of the Methodist movement. These earnest young men caused a sensation at Oxford by frequently meeting together for Bible study, Communion, and prayer. They were derisively referred to as the "Holy Club," "Sacramentarians," "Bible moths" (feeding on the Bible as moths on cloth), "Bible bigots," and "Methodists." John was called the "curator" or "father" of the Holy Club. Charles had started the group while John was away serving at Wroote. Charles said that they were given the name *Methodist* because of their strict conformity to the method of biblical study prescribed by the university. John would later redefine this term in his *English Dictionary* as "one that lives according to the *method* laid down in the Bible. The Methodist controversy eventually cost Wesley the loss of earnings, friends, and reputation, but he still insisted that it was worth it in order to gain a pure heart.

That same year the Holy Club began to dissolve when John, Charles, and two others of its members sailed for the American colony of Georgia. John was to serve as missionary to the native Americans and pastor of the Savannah parish, but a failed romance with Sophia Hopkey, niece of the chief magistrate of Savannah, contributed to the failure of this endeavor. In addition, although Wesley had faithfully served his flock, he exhibited a high churchmanship that antagonized the parish. Eventually Wesley left Georgia and returned to England.

Though Wesley's ministry in America was less than successful, an experience on his voyage to Georgia dramatically impacted his later work. During a violent storm, Wesley was cowering in fear of death, but he noticed a group of Moravian Brethren who were remarkably calm. An interview with the Moravians' leader upon landing in Georgia set in motion Wesley's search for the living reality of the doctrines he preached.

On January 24, 1738, shortly after his return from Georgia, Wesley wrote in his *Journal*: "I went to America to convert the Indians; but O! who shall convert me? Who, what is he that shall deliver me from this evil heart of unbelief? . . . O who will deliver me from this fear of death?"

Back in London John met Peter Bohler, a Moravian, who instructed him that salvation comes by faith. Wesley also read Luther's commentary on Galatians, which emphasizes justification by faith alone. Then Wesley attended a Moravian meeting in May of 1738, near his old school, Charterhouse. There he experienced what he described as a strange warming of his heart. He came to believe that he was indeed forgiven of his sin and had received salvation from the law of sin and death.

Eighteen days after Wesley's experience at Charterhouse, John preached at Oxford University his famous sermon "By Grace Ye Are Saved through Faith." This became the theme of his life thereafter.

Wesley immediately left for Germany, where he visited the Moravian Brethren leader Count Zinzendorf. He returned to England in September 1738, joining Charles in preaching the gospel wherever they were permitted. The Anglican congregations soon closed their doors to the Wesleys because of their enthusiasm, but they were invited to the religious societies that existed within the Church of England. In May 1738 they had founded their own "little society" on Fetter Lane, London. By autumn the Fetter Lane society numbered fifty-six men and eight women.

Encouraged by the Great Awakening in New England and by George Whitefield's successes at outdoor preaching, Wesley began preaching in fields at Bristol (1739). This sparked the great Methodist revival in England. During the following fifty years, John Wesley rode 250,000 miles on the roads of England, Scotland, and Ireland to preach 42,000 sermons. He also published 233 books. His tireless and incessant activity changed the face of British society forever.

In 1739 Wesley bought and renovated an abandoned cannon foundry near London. Seating fifteen hundred, the foundry served as Methodist headquarters for thirty-eight years until, in 1777, City Road Chapel was built.

John Wesley's unique practical genius can be seen in his ability to organize. Wesley's Methodist societies stand as a testament to his work in evangelism. He published *Rules* for the Methodist societies in 1743 to avoid the scandal of unworthy members. In 1744 the societies imitated the early church in holding love feasts and broke new ground by gathering in the first annual conference. This gathering of preachers at Wesley's invitation developed into a sort of parliament, deciding doctrinal and administrative questions. The conference perpetuated Wesley's authority among the British Methodists after his death.

The Methodist revival caused a great tumult in England. Rioting mobs often threatened the lives of Wesley and his followers. Methodism eventually emerged as an evangelical order within the Church of England, though it was never appreciated or approved by the church hierarchy. Church doors continued to be closed to Wesley's teaching. Nevertheless, Wesley was a member of the Church of England until his death. He refused to schedule Methodist meetings to conflict with Anglican services.

Wesley broke the mold of the settled Anglican curate and became an extensively itinerant preacher. Most ordained clergymen of the day had no taste for this approach to the ministry. So Wesley was forced to enlist a band of dedicated layworkers who also became itinerant preachers and administrators of the Methodist societies. These Methodist "circuit riders" became an important element in American life after the American Revolution.

In 1770 Wesley sent Francis Asbury to America to strengthen and enlarge the societies there, and in 1772 Wesley ordained Thomas Coke as general superintendent of the Methodists in America. Coke then ordained Asbury. This development horrified Charles, who said that his brother had "assumed the episcopal character." John later ordained several others "to administer the sacraments of baptism and the Lord's Supper according to the usage of the Church of England." Yet Wesley continued to hold that Methodism was simply a society of Christians who would remain loyal to their own church or denomination.

John Wesley's tireless work did reap some negative consequences, however. His marriage suffered as a result of his busy lifestyle, and his wife, Maria, resented the regimen he followed in his work. In 1771 she left without warning. Attempts at reconciliation were made, but when his wife was buried on October 12, 1781, John had not even heard of her death.

Among Wesley's many books were educational treatises, translations from Greek, Latin, and Hebrew, histories of Rome and England, an ecclesiastical history, and biblical commentaries. He edited *Imitation of Christ* and works by Bunyan, Baxter, Edwards, Rutherford, and Law. He compiled an English dictionary, published twenty-three collections of hymns, and recorded his activities, travels, and spiritual life in his *Journal* (1735–1790). His medical handbook, *Primitive Physick,* went through twenty-three editions in his lifetime and nine after his death.

Beginning in the days of the Holy Club until his death, Wesley was concerned "to reform the nation." He pioneered or participated in many causes of his day: legal and prison reform, civil rights, popular education, and abolition of slavery. Wesley's last act was to dictate a letter to William Wilberforce, who was fighting in Parliament to abolish the slave trade.

At ten o'clock on Wednesday morning, March 2, 1791, John Wesley passed into eternity. Thousands filed by his open coffin in City Road Chapel. Memorial services were held throughout England, Scotland, and Ireland, and newspapers and magazines published scores of sermons and articles. At the funeral John Whitehead echoed the hearts of millions of mourners as he lamented, "Know ye not that there is a prince and a great man fallen this day in Israel?" (2 Samuel 3:38, KJV).

John Wesley's *Journal* has been collected into eight large volumes. In it are found his thoughts and experiences on a wide variety of topics, revealing the practical devotional life of a great Christian leader.

In his *Journal* Wesley writes freely of his various experiences. He recorded the story of his conversion at a meeting on Aldersgate Street, London. He reveals his experience and dependence on the presence of God in everyday life. He describes his understanding of faith as one of the gifts of the Spirit and asserts that a person must "have some degree of it before all things in him are become new" (December 31, 1739). Wesley details his experiences with the gift of healing and often describes various miracles and prophecies.

Wesley's *Journal* chronicles how his spirituality evidenced itself in practical approaches to social concerns. He addressed such topics as tax paying, conscription, slavery, and the American Revolution. He was always concerned with employing the poor. Wesley also testified to his pioneering role in advocating the education of children.

From his experience at Aldersgate, Wesley never ceased to advocate the fullness of life in Christ. He continually struggled to desire heavenly reward rather than earthly riches. And so John Wesley's heart still influences others through his personal *Journal.*

The New Testament in the Original Greek 1881
B. F. Westcott and J. F. Hort

Brooke Foss Westcott, born in 1825, was raised in Birmingham, England. He later attended Trinity College, Cambridge, where he became a fellow in 1849. During his university days he befriended J. B. Lightfoot and F. J. Hort, and together they produced some of the best Christian scholarship of the nineteenth century. Beginning in 1853, Westcott and Hort worked together to produce *The New Testament in the Original Greek* (1881).

In 1870 Westcott was appointed regius professor of divinity at Cambridge, and in 1890 he succeeded Lightfoot as bishop of Durham. Westcott had a deep concern for the social and industrial problems of his diocese, and on several occasions he helped the coal miners there.

In addition to his commentaries on John, Hebrews, and the Epistles of John, which have become classics in their own right, Westcott wrote a *History of the New Testament Canon* and *A History of the English Bible.* He also served on the committee that produced the English Revised Version.

John Fenton Hort was born in Dublin, Ireland, in 1828. He was educated at Rugby and then at Trinity College, Cambridge, becoming a fellow in 1852. Eventually, Hort became Hulsean professor of divinity at Cambridge. He taught there for most of his life and became closely associated with J. B. Lightfoot and B. F. Westcott.

Hort, along with Westcott and Lightfoot, had planned to collaborate on writing a commentary on all the books of the New Testament, but they never fully realized their collective goal. Lightfoot completed commentaries on some Pauline Epistles; Westcott completed his work on Hebrews, John, and the Epistles of John. Hort did not publish any books before he died. Most of his time was invested in the English Revised Version, and he was known to be a perfectionist. After his death, however, it was discovered that he had written commentaries on James and 1 Peter. A dozen of Hort's works were published posthumously; some of these works include *Judaistic Christianity* (1894), *The Christian Ecclesia* (1897), and his Hulsean Lectures of 1871, which dealt with philosophical theology. In addition to being a brilliant biblical scholar, he was also an involved churchman. He was particularly interested in social issues and supported the work of F. D. Maurice and Charles Kingsley, both leaders in the British social gospel movement.

Westcott and Hort's *The New Testament in the Original Greek* is an eclectic text compiled from the texts of the best New Testament manuscripts available at the time. Their work, which took twenty-eight years to complete, is greatly indebted to the labors of other scholars, especially the textual critics Tregelles and Tischendorf. Samuel Tregelles devoted his entire life to publishing a single Greek text of the New Testament (which came out in six parts, from 1857 to 1872). Tregelles's text is based on the assumption that the texts of the earliest known manuscripts are to be preferred. During this same era, Constantin Tischendorf devoted a lifetime of labor to discovering more New Testament manuscripts and producing more accurate editions of the Greek New Testament.

Along with their New Testament text, Westcott and Hort published an introduction detailing the theory behind their textual decisions. They believed that two major manuscripts, Codex Vaticanus and Codex Sinaiticus, most closely represent the original New Testament text. They used these two manuscripts to create a base text and then made small changes to this text on the basis of other early manuscript evidence. By this method, they hoped to provide a text that was as close to the original New Testament as possible. Their theory was revolutionary, and their text was responsible for overthrowing long-term allegiance to the *Textus Receptus,* the Greek text that was derived from Erasmus's text and used to translate the King James Version.

Westcott and Hort's textual theories and New Testament text have influenced textual studies for the past one hundred years. Most English Bible translations of the first part of the twentieth century (including the American Standard Version) were based on the Westcott and Hort text. The primary New Testament texts today (Nestle-Aland's *Novum Testamentum Graece,* 27th edition; United Bible Society's *Greek New Testament,* 4th edition) bear great resemblance to the text edited by Westcott and Hort.

Abide in Christ   c. 1895
Andrew Murray
. . . .

Born in Cape Town, South Africa, in 1828, Andrew Murray became a noted missionary leader. His father was a Scottish Presbyterian serving the Dutch Reformed Church of South Africa, and his mother had connections with both French Huguenots and German Lutherans. Murray was educated at Aberdeen University, Scotland, and Utrecht University in the Netherlands. After ordination in 1848, he served pastorates at Bloemfontein,

Worcester, Cape Town, and Wellington. He helped to found the University College of the Orange Free State and the Stellenbosch Seminary. He served as Moderator of the Cape Synod of the Dutch Reformed Church and was president of both the YMCA (1865) and the South Africa General Mission (1888–1917), now the Africa Evangelical Fellowship.

Murray was one of the chief promoters of missions in South Africa. This led to the Dutch Reformed Church missions to nationals in the Transvaal and Malawi. Apart from his evangelistic tours in South Africa, he spoke at the Keswick and Northfield Conventions in 1895, making a great impression upon his British and American audiences. For his contribution to world missions he was given an honorary doctorate by the universities of Aberdeen (1898) and Cape of Good Hope (1907).

Murray is best known today for his devotional writings, which place great emphasis on the need for a rich, personal devotional life. Many of his 240 publications convey his thoughts about this devotion and its outworking in the life of the Christian. Several of his books have become devotional classics; among these are *Abide in Christ, Absolute Surrender, With Christ in the School of Prayer, The Spirit of Christ,* and *Waiting on God.*

Andrew Murray published *Abide in Christ* "with the desire to help those who have not yet fully understood what the Saviour meant [by the command 'abide in me'], or who have feared that it was a life beyond their reach." The book is a series of daily meditations designed to be read over one month. Each day's reading features an aspect of Christ's message in John 15:1-11, which describes Christ as the true vine and believers as the branches.

Abide in Christ is a beginner's guidebook for a life in Christ. Murray opens by pointing out that Jesus' invitation, "Come to me" in Matthew 11:28 is logically completed by his command in John 15:4, "Abide in me." In other words, he is saying, "Come to me, and stay with me." Murray explains that the rest that is found by taking Christ's yoke is the result of abiding in Christ. The parable of the branch and the vine in John 15 describes the nature and completeness of the union into which Christ invites believers. The purpose of this union, according to Murray, "is for fruit, much fruit."

Andrew Murray has designed this classic of Christian devotion to include the entire experience of Christ. The title of each daily reading provides a hint of Murray's intent and message for that day. He begins with Jesus' call to follow him and ends with Christ's return for those he has called.

In His Steps 1896
Charles Sheldon

Charles Sheldon was born in Wellsville, New York, in 1857. He was educated at Phillips Academy, Andover (1879), Brown University (1883), and Andover Theological Seminary (1886). Sheldon's first pastorate was at the Congregational Church of Waterbury, Vermont, where he served from 1886 to 1889. He then moved to Topeka, Kansas, to become the minister of the newly founded Central Community Church, where he remained until 1919. From 1920 to 1925 he was editor in chief of the *Christian Herald,* continuing thereafter as contributing editor.

Sheldon wrote more than fifty books, most of them inspirational works regarding current social and religious issues. His best-known work is *In His Steps* (1896), which has sold more than 6 million copies.

Sheldon was an active participant in the Prohibition movement. From 1914 to 1915 he was a member of the "Flying Squad" that spoke on behalf of Prohibition in 247 American churches in the course of 243 days.

In his classic devotional novel, *In His Steps,* Charles Sheldon recounts the experiences of volunteers who pledge for one year to continually ask the question "What would Jesus do?" before doing anything. First published in 1897, *In His Steps* is one of the most widely read religious novels ever written. Since the book is now public domain, it is impossible to track the number of copies in print, but estimates range from 6 to 8 million copies or more.

While a young minister in Topeka, Kansas, Sheldon once disguised himself as an unemployed printer living on the streets. He was shocked at the indifference shown to him by the city's Christians. Sheldon's opens with a similar scenario—a homeless man happens into a Sunday church service and asks the congregation, "What do you mean when you sing, 'I'll go with Him, with Him, all the way?' Do you mean that you are suffering and denying yourselves and trying to save lost, suffering humanity just as I understand Jesus did?" The man then collapses and dies. This sets in motion the events of *In His Steps,* which Charles Sheldon wrote to be read aloud to his Topeka congregation.

The novel tracks the lives of several church members who agree to live in response to the question "What would Jesus do?" This question profoundly impacts many lives all over the fictional city of Raymond. Among those devoted to such discipleship are a newspaper editor, a young heiress and her brother, a railroad executive, a singer of national reputation, and a college president. The movement soon overflows the confines of both the church and the city of Raymond. It eventually spreads to a prominent church in Chicago, where even a bishop is affected.

In His Steps is an engaging Christian novel that is enjoyable to read. Through the fictitious pastor Henry Maxwell, Sheldon communicates his dream for "the regeneration of Christendom," with believers "following Him all the way, walking obediently in His steps."

The Twentieth Century

A Theology for the Social Gospel 1917
Walter Rauschenbusch

. . . .

Rauschenbusch was born in Rochester, New York, where his father was a professor in the German Department of the Baptist Theological Seminary. Rauschenbusch lived in Rochester most of his life, attending college and seminary there and teaching for his last twenty-one years in the seminary. His one lengthy excursion from Rochester, however, changed his life forever.

In 1886 Rauschenbusch became pastor of the Second German Baptist Church in New York City. The church was largely made up of immigrants who lived on New York's lower East Side, an area aptly called "Hell's Kitchen." There Rauschenbusch saw the immigrants' sordid living conditions, labor exploitation by industrial giants, and governmental indifference to the suffering of the poor. This led to a personal revolution for Rauschenbusch. In looking back on this time, Rauschenbusch noted, "I began to work in New York, and there, among the working people, . . . I began to understand the connection between religious and social questions." Rauschenbusch asked himself if his Christian heritage had anything to offer the suffering thousands in the immediate vicinity of his church. His question forced him to rethink his religious categories and to begin a fresh new study of the Bible. It also encouraged him to explore the views of contemporary dynamic social critics.

Rauschenbusch left New York City in 1897 to return to Rochester, but these experiences formed the context out of which his first book, *Christianity and the Social Crisis* (1907), was written. This volume became an immediate sensation and catapulted Rauschenbusch to national prominence as a spokesman for a socially committed Christianity. The book noted the great interest Old Testament prophets had shown in social matters and how socially powerful the life of the early church had been. It also called for a faith that joined Christian beliefs with social ethics. Yet the book revealed Rauschenbusch's continuing evangelical sentiments: "In personal religion the first requirement is to repent and believe the gospel"; at the same time, however, it made provocative new statements: "Social religions, too, demand repentance and faith: repentance for our social sins; faith in the possibility of a new social order."

In subsequent books, Rauschenbusch fleshed out his picture of a "social gospel." His *Prayers for the Social Awakening* (1910) has been described as a modern devotional classic. The prayers also reflect the combined reliance upon Christian faith and human potential that characterized much of the early social gospel. *Christianizing the Social Order* (1912) contained Rauschenbusch's most sustained criticism of American capitalism. It was, according to Rauschenbusch, blinded to human needs by its competitiveness and its drive for profit. Its major firms tyrannized the weak and defenseless; it fostered values through advertising and the mass market that debased the spiritual qualities of life. In the place of capitalism, Rauschenbusch called for a social order characterized by justice, collective ownership of most property, democracy in the organization of industry, and a much more equal distribution of goods. Rauschenbusch frequently called himself a Christian socialist, but he also took pains to disavow Marxist or doctrinaire formulas for overhauling American economic life.

Rauschenbusch's last major work, *A Theology for the Social Gospel* (1917), appeared shortly before his death. This influential volume set out systematically what a Christian theology would look like if it took seriously the needs of modern society. It was somewhat less optimistic than earlier books about the possibilities for human improvement. Yet Rauschenbusch had always been the one leader of the social gospel who had never underestimated the reality of evil or its permanent roots in the human heart. The volume also warned of how dangerous mere social movements could be if they lost the backing of Christian theology.

Rauschenbusch was an "evangelical liberal" who combined many elements of orthodoxy with many convictions of the modern age. His reputation as the leader of the *social* gospel, however, has blinded both liberals and evangelicals to how much orthodoxy remained in his social *gospel.* Specific evaluation of Rauschenbusch aside, he was undoubtedly the most influential American Christian thinker in the first third of the twentieth century.

"We have a social gospel. We need a systematic theology large enough to match it and vital enough to back it." This challenge is taken up by Walter Rauschenbusch in *A Theology for the Social Gospel.* First given in 1917 as the Nathaniel W. Taylor Lectures at Yale University, *A Theology for the Social Gospel* is not itself that systematic theology. Rather, its first chapters "show that a readjustment and expansion of theology . . . [are] necessary, feasible, desirable, and legitimate." Rauschenbusch saw such an adjusted theology as the intellectual basis for the social gospel.

His work treats the subject with serious and scholarly study while remaining vivid and moving as well.

The main portion of the book proposes concrete suggestions for readjusting doctrinal theology in order to make room for the religious convictions of the social gospel. Rauschenbusch evaded many aspects of theology, however, and focused the six central chapters of the book on sin, its transmission from generation to generation, and its incorporation into an almost intractable "kingdom of evil." While the doctrine of original sin addresses the transmission of sin, Rauschenbusch said, "Many modern theologians are ready to abandon this doctrine." He, on the other hand, took "pleasure [in] defending it." Against this kingdom of evil, Rauschenbusch proposed a theology for advancing the "kingdom of God," a concept he borrowed from the New Testament Gospels.

A major theological contribution of A Theology for the Social Gospel is Rauschenbusch's assertion that "sin is essentially selfishness." Rauschenbusch believed that sin occurs when people seek their own profit over the welfare of others. He believed this worked directly against the kingdom of God. For Rauschenbusch, "the chief significance of the social gospel for the doctrine of sin [is that] it revives the vision of the kingdom of God."

Rauschenbusch also insisted that religion and ethics must be viewed as "inseparable elements of the same single-minded and wholehearted life, in which the consciousness of God and the consciousness of humanity blend completely." This was the mind-set of the prophets of the Bible.

In A Theology for the Social Gospel, Rauschenbusch reexamines many classic doctrinal questions of Christianity. He reinterprets them in light of his concern for social justice. Concerning the doctrine of the person of Christ, Rauschenbusch asserts, "The speculative problem of Christological dogma was how the divine and human natures united in the one person of Christ; the problem of the social gospel is how the divine life of Christ can get control of human society. The social gospel is concerned about a progressive social incarnation of God."

Walter Rauschenbusch possessed true confidence in his vision for the gospel. As he penned the final words of *A Theology for the Social Gospel* at the beginning of the twentieth century, he wrote, "The era of prophetic and democratic Christianity has just begun. This concerns the social gospel, for the social gospel is the voice of prophecy in modern life." Many social leaders who came after him, including Martin Luther King Jr., agreed.

Church Dogmatics   c. 1932
Karl Barth
. . . .

Karl Barth was born in Basel, Switzerland, in 1886. His father was a pastor and professor of New Testament and church history in a school related to the Swiss Reformed Church. Barth received his early schooling in Bern, where he showed an interest in military affairs, history, and drama. Following European custom, he studied at several universities: Bern, Berlin, Tübingen, and Marburg. At Bern he was introduced to Immanuel Kant's philosophy and Friedrich Schleiermacher's theology. In time Barth went on to study with the leading neo-Kantian theologian Wilhelm Herrmann of Marburg. Barth first studied at Berlin, however, where he was influenced by church historian Adolf von Harnack. To honor his father's wishes, Barth then went to Tübingen to study with a conservative New Testament theologian, Adolf Schlatter. Finally, in 1908, Barth went to Marburg. He later considered Herrmann's teaching the greatest single influence of his student days.

Barth's training was typical of early twentieth-century German theology with its emphasis on humanity rather than divinity.

Many German theologians believed that God's purposes were carried out solely through the events of human history and that humans had the capacity for ever-increasing progress in society.

In 1913 Barth married Nelly Hoffmann, and they eventually had five sons, one of whom, Markus, became internationally known for biblical and theological scholarship.

Barth was ordained in the Swiss Reformed Church. He served one pastorate for two years in Geneva and a second for ten years in the small town of Safenwil. There Barth struggled throughout the years of World War I to teach his congregation how to apply the Bible's message to complex modern life. Initially he rejected a conservative emphasis on personal salvation in favor of a liberal stress on social change. Barth even joined a socialist political party.

In August 1914 the Western world was on the edge of total war, and Barth's respected teachers were supporting their nation's military aims. If this was where German liberal theology inevitably led, however, Barth could not join with them. He believed this represented a failure of German liberal theology to answer crucial modern questions. Turning to a fresh study of the Bible, Barth began to construct a whole new theological system in order to address these questions. In this new system, the "Word of God," which could be found within the Bible, describes a God who, solely in grace, seeks to redeem humankind. In 1917 Karl Barth and Eduard Thurneysen copublished a book of sermons entitled *Seek God and You Shall Live*.

Barth studied the apostle Paul's letters, preparing manuscripts on Romans, Ephesians, and 2 Corinthians. In 1918 Barth's commentary on Romans was published, marking the beginning of Barth's departure from his liberal theological training. With a completely revised second edition in 1921, his break with liberalism was complete. He then challenged contemporary theology by emphasizing God's complete difference (transcendence) from humanity. Because of this transcendence, Barth maintained, people need a revelation from God if he is to be known and obeyed.

Barth gradually refined his thought, developing a total theological system. In it he emphasized God's holiness, his incomprehensibility to the human mind, and his sovereign grace. Barth's early expressions of his "new orthodoxy" were strongly influenced by the Danish philosopher Søren Kierkegaard and the Russian novelist Fyodor Dostoyevsky, as well as by a rediscovery of the Reformation emphasis upon God's grace.

Barth's new approach was soon taken up by a number of other young theologians, including Emil Brunner, Rudolf Bultmann, and Friedrich Gogarten. Barth eventually differed with these theologians on various issues, but their "new beginning" completely reshaped twentieth-century biblical interpretation. Barth taught his theology at several European universities: Göttingen (1921–1925), Münster (1925–1930), Bonn (1930–1935), and Basel (1935–1962).

When Adolf Hitler and National Socialism (Nazism) came to power in Germany in 1933, Barth and Thurneysen published a series of pamphlets entitled *Theological Existence Today* to oppose Hitler's cultural perversion of the Christian faith. By 1934 Barth was a leader in the German movement known as the Confessing Church. He was the major framer of its statement of faith, the Barmen Declaration. Such activities forced him to flee in 1935 to Basel, where, in addition to his new teaching responsibilities, he served in the Swiss army as a border guard. At the war's end Barth advocated Allied openness to helping the German people, a seeming turnaround that brought sharp criticism from some of his colleagues.

The majority of Barth's life was spent teaching and writing, with some public lecturing and preaching. His major writings include a commentary on Romans, *Church Dogmatics* (a multivolume systematic theology of nearly seventy-five hundred pages), *The Word of God and the Word of Man* (1928), *Evangelical Theology* (1963), and *The Humanity of God* (1960). In 1937 he gave the Gifford Lectures at Aberdeen (Scotland), and in 1962 he lectured in America at Princeton Theological Seminary and the University of Chicago. During the decade before his retirement in 1962, Barth often preached to inmates in Basel's prison.

Barth's greatest influence was theological, with his emphasis on God's sovereignty placing him firmly in the Reformed (Calvinistic) tradition. He differed radically from the mainstream of continental European theology, rejecting both its subjective emphasis on religious experience and the prevalent idea that Christian doctrine is subject to, or limited by, its historical origins. By reaffirming what Kierkegaard had called an "infinite qualitative difference" between God and humankind, Barth rescued theology from captivity to anthropology—that is, he reasserted God's reality and sovereignty over human knowledge or imagination.

One characteristic of Barth's developed theology was his rejection of "natural theology." In a crucial debate with his friend Emil Brunner (published in 1934), he contended that all human efforts to define God by means of natural observation end in idolatry. Barth stressed the crippling effect of sin on human reason, rendering humans incapable of comprehending God's message apart from his redeeming grace. People will come to God only through faith in God's self-revelation.

Because Barth accepted certain higher critical views of Scripture, he refused to equate the Bible directly with God's inspired Word. Inspiration, for Barth, had more to do with the Bible reader than with either the Bible itself or its writers. The words of the Bible convey the "Word of God" as the Holy Spirit speaks through them to the reader. Perhaps more than any other aspect of Barth's theology, his doctrine of Scripture created serious misgivings among many evangelical theologians.

Following Calvin, Barth insisted that true knowledge of God comes in obedience to God. Jesus' devotion to doing God's will and his call to discipleship provided the model of obedient service.

Barth's "neoorthodox" theology strengthened many Christian leaders in Europe, giving them a basis for standing against persecution. But its lack of objective criteria for judgment in theological matters created severe problems for its adherents. Some of the "death of God" theologians in the 1960s began as followers of Barth. Near the end of his career, Barth considered *Humanity of God* a corrective balance to his earlier radical stress on God's transcendence. Nevertheless, he insisted that his earlier theology was appropriate for the crisis in which it first appeared.

Karl Barth began to write *Church Dogmatics* in 1932 and continued the work for the rest of his life. His dogmatic benchmark is that all we know and say about God and about humanity is controlled by our knowledge of Jesus Christ as "true God and true man." Barth considered that he stood in the tradition of Irenaeus and Athanasius, early church fathers who argued against heresy, and of the reformers Luther and Calvin. His life was devoted to a dialogue with liberal Protestantism on the left and Roman Catholicism on the right. Both sides, he felt, had moved away from the Bible's emphasis that God accepts us only by grace in Jesus Christ.

Church Dogmatics was planned in five volumes. At his death Barth had not completed volume 5. It was to cover the doctrine of redemption—the events of the last days and the second coming of Jesus Christ. In the four completed books, Barth discusses the four intersecting areas of Christian doctrine: the Word of God, God, creation, and redemption. Volume 1, focusing on the Word of God, addresses the topics of the Trinity, Christology, and Holy Scripture. Volume 2 provides a more specific study of the doctrine of God. This volume discusses human knowledge of God, the attributes of God, predestination, and Christian ethics.

Volume 3 covers the doctrine of creation. Barth insists that knowledge of true humanity is disclosed solely in Jesus Christ. Since humans are sinners and pervert their real, created nature, Christ shows humans in proper relationship with God. Barth addresses the concepts of providence, nothingness, and angels. Barth also discusses certain ethical questions, such as sexuality, marriage, humankind's relationship with animals, capital punishment, and war.

In volume 4, Barth's discussion of reconciliation forms the heart of his *Church Dogmatics*. Two facets of this work are accomplished simultaneously in the life, death, and resurrection of Jesus Christ, the God-man. The first was accomplished as Jesus Christ became a servant in order to do the work of atonement. The second is found in humankind's fellowship with God through Jesus Christ the servant. Both of these facets are accomplished in the person of Jesus Christ.

Barth also explains how Christ's work is made certain by the Holy Spirit's work of calling the church and awakening individual hope. The church is composed of people who, through the power of the Holy Spirit, have faith in God through the person and work of Jesus Christ. Those who belong to the church bear witness to the world that Jesus Christ is Lord and Savior.

My Utmost for His Highest   1935
Oswald Chambers

Oswald Chambers was born in Aberdeen, Scotland, in 1874. He was the son of a Baptist preacher and became a believer under the preaching of Charles Spurgeon. Chambers studied art in London and Edinburgh but abandoned a promising career to train for the Baptist ministry at Dunoon College.

Most of the public ministry of Oswald Chambers was with the Pentecostal League of Prayer, especially after the League's founder died in 1909. Chambers visited Holiness camps in the United States and Japan before becoming principal of the Bible Training College in London. With his wife, Gertrude, and his daughter he ministered to British troops in Egypt. It was here that a sudden illness took his life. More than forty titles of Chambers's works have been published posthumously, the most popular being *My Utmost for His Highest*.

Oswald Chambers's devotional classic *My Utmost for His Highest* is the most widely read book of its kind. Compiled by his wife from her notes of his sermons in London and Egypt, *My Utmost* was published in 1935. Since then it has sold millions of copies and is still enjoyed today. A popular edition with carefully updated terminology and language has recently been published.

After an introduction by Gertrude Chambers, *My Utmost for His Highest* consists of 365 readings, each assigned a date from January 1 through December 31. Each reading bears its own title and begins with a verse of Scripture. Chambers then addresses a topic related to the verse of the day. Verses are selected from almost every New Testament book, and many come from the Old Testament as well. In the Old Testament Chambers quotes mostly from Genesis, Psalms, and Isaiah. In the New Testament, special attention is given to the Gospels of Matthew and John, with seventy-two readings being taken from the Gospel of John alone.

The subjects covered in *My Utmost* span a wide range of spiritual and practical concerns. These include drudgery, friendship with God, introspection, laziness, and moods. Redemption is discussed in twenty-two readings, and spiritual ambition is covered in over fifty.

Gertrude Chambers's desire for *My Utmost* was that readers would be refreshed each day by the Holy Spirit. There is little doubt that this goal has been accomplished millions of times over in the lives of its readers.

The Cost of Discipleship   1937
Dietrich Bonhoeffer

. . . .

Dietrich Bonhoeffer and his twin sister, Sabine, were born in 1906 in Breslau (now Wroclaw, Poland). Dietrich's father was the foremost neurologist and psychiatrist teaching at the University of Berlin; his mother was the granddaughter of Karl von Hase, a nineteenth-century church historian. At the age of seventeen, Dietrich began theological studies at Tübingen. He also enrolled at the University of Berlin, where he took additional theological studies under Adolf von Harnack.

Bonhoeffer qualified for the licentiate under Reinhold Seeberg with a work entitled *The Communion of Saints*. This creative study brought the structures of society (sociology) under the judgment of Scripture and addressed the topic of the church in society. At the age of twenty-four, Bonhoeffer qualified for teaching at the University of Berlin with the presentation of his work *Act and Being*. Building on his first work, Bonhoeffer spoke of God's being found in the Word and realized in real-life situations. He asserted that Christ lived in the community of believers. Bonhoeffer's two early philosophical/theological books provide the basic structure for his later books, which are generally biblical, ethical, and personal in character.

Bonhoeffer's two most widely read books are *The Cost of Discipleship* and *Letters and Papers from Prison*. Among these writings, the key focus is Bonhoeffer's interpretation of Christ and his "body," the church on earth. As his theology developed further, Bonhoeffer asserted that Jesus Christ is Lord over the body (the church) as well. He also addresses Jesus Christ in relation to the whole world. The core of Bonhoeffer's theology is given a practical turn in *Ethics,* in which he states that God, in Christ, reveals himself through concrete moral decisions in the secular world.

While studying at Union Theological Seminary in New York City (1930–1931), Bonhoeffer team-taught a Sunday school class at a church in Harlem. This experience proved to be a powerful lesson on how "enslaved" people could endure dehumanizing oppression by exercising simple, biblical faith, particularly in praise and worship. Bonhoeffer later returned to Germany.

When many pastors were yielding to Hitler's interference in church affairs, Bonhoeffer resisted and helped create the Confessing Church in Germany. In 1935 he began and led an "illegal" seminary in Finkenwalde. From the earliest days of the Nazi regime, Bonhoeffer identified himself with the resistance movement against Adolf Hitler, who in 1933 had become the dictator of Germany. On November 9, 1938, Bonhoeffer witnessed "Kristallnacht," when over six hundred synagogues were destroyed, seventy-five hundred Jewish shops were looted, and thirty-five thousand Jews were arrested. This led Bonhoeffer and other conspirators to intensify their efforts against the Nazi regime; they plotted to kill Hitler in order to end Nazi power. Bonhoeffer was eventually arrested in April 1943 and hung in 1944, shortly after the plot to kill Hitler failed.

Published in 1937, *The Cost of Discipleship* established Dietrich Bonhoeffer as a theologian of high distinction. With this work, Bonhoeffer reaffirms the concept of faith in the Christian life. As he reaffirms faith, Bonhoeffer emphasizes the Word (the Scriptures), the sacraments (baptism and the Lord's Supper), and the earthly community of faith (the church). The book's title in German is simply *Discipleship,* since Bonhoeffer takes faith, justification, and sanctification (the pillars of reformed theology) and unites them into the single concept of discipleship.

The key formula of his work is "only he who believes is obedient, and only he who is obedient believes." Bonhoeffer claims that this theorem revalidates the complete premise of justification and restores its true value. But Bonhoeffer was always inclined to emphasize the community of faith as well. In *The Cost of Discipleship* Bonhoeffer insists that "it is impossible to become a new man as a solitary individual. . . . It means the church, the body of Christ, in fact it means Christ himself." This does not mean, however, that discipleship should become a world movement or creed; nor is discipleship an ideology or technique since these require measurable results. To Bonhoeffer, right Christology requires a person to be called and to follow. Those who do this "are ready to suffer with the Word."

The Cost of Discipleship is divided into four chapters. The opening chapter challenges the reader with a discourse on grace and discipleship. Bonhoeffer attacks the "cheap grace" that was being preached in the churches of his time; he counters this easy believism by asserting, "When Christ calls a man, he bids him come and die."

Chapter 2 further develops Bonhoeffer's discussion of discipleship as it examines Jesus Christ's demands on the believer in the Sermon on the Mount. Chapter 3 discusses spreading this message of Jesus Christ, and chapter 4 addresses the believer and his or her relationship to the church, the body of Christ on earth.

In this classic work, Bonhoeffer describes a disciple's life as simple and carefree. This simplicity is rooted in the disciple's obedience to one master, which sets the disciple free from other concerns. The truth of this work is reinforced by the real-life example of Bonhoeffer himself.

The Nature and Destiny of Man   1941
Reinhold Niebuhr

. . . .

Reinhold Niebuhr was born in Missouri in 1893. His father was a pastor in the German Evangelical Church. Niebuhr remained with this small denomination as it moved into the Evangelical and Reformed Church and eventually into the United Church of Christ. He attended his denomination's college and seminary (Elmhurst and Eden) before doing two years of graduate work at Yale. In 1915 he accepted the pastorate of Bethel Evangelical Church in Detroit, where he served for thirteen years. It was in this church that Niebuhr came of age theologically as his liberalism encountered the harsh realities of industrial America. He was particularly upset with what industrial life did to the laborers. He wondered what hope there was for American civilization when "naive gentlemen with a genius for mechanics suddenly become the arbiters over the lives and fortunes of hundreds of thousands." While still in Detroit, Niebuhr began to advocate radical solutions to the human crisis as he saw it. He proposed socialism and pacifism for life in society and a new "Christian Realism" for theology.

When Niebuhr moved to New York's Union Theological Seminary in 1928, he carried with him the commitments formed in Detroit. The coming of World War II led him to abandon his socialism and pacifism, but he remained a dedicated social activist, serving on scores of committees in the 1930s and 1940s. He helped to form Americans for Democratic Action and New York's Liberal Party, edited the journal *Christianity and Crisis,* and wrote prolifically for newspapers and magazines.

Niebuhr's theological ethics were developed more systematically in a long list of major books. The two most important are *Moral Man and Immoral Society* (1932) and *The Nature and Destiny of Man* (1941, 1943). The first severely criticized the liberal optimism concerning humanity. It gave a sharp rebuke to the notion that human beings were perfectible as individuals and inherently good in groups. The second work provided a more systematic discussion of the nature of humanity and how it affects life in the world.

Niebuhr's neoorthodoxy was quite different from that of the European continent. It was more concerned with ethics than with theology proper; it focused more on the doctrine of humanity than on the doctrine of God; and it showed more concern for life in society than for life in the church. Nonetheless, it shared the conviction of European neoorthodoxy that liberalism had placed too much faith in humanity and too little reliance on God.

Niebuhr showed little interest in the doctrines of Christ or grace except where they aided his study of humanity. It could be said that he was more interested in the paradoxes of human life than in salvation offered through Christ. Likewise, Niebuhr seemed to use Scripture more because it was relevant to the modern condition than because it was God's Word to humankind. Nevertheless, Niebuhr does share an evangelical understanding of humankind as fallen and in need of divine help.

Reinhold Niebuhr published *The Nature and Destiny of Man* in two volumes, releasing the first in 1941 and the second in 1943. These volumes were compiled from his speeches at the Gifford Lectures in 1939 (University of Aberdeen, Scotland).

The first, and most significant, volume, addressing the topic of human nature, is a systematic discussion of what Niebuhr believed to be humankind's most basic problem—sinfulness. Niebuhr assesses past views of human nature and contrasts them with the biblical view. He then reasserts the biblical view of human nature in modern terms and concepts. Niebuhr uses the biblical story of creation to explain humanity's potential for both true good and radical evil. Because humans are made in the image of God, they are good; but their finiteness can lead to evil results if humans overstep their bounds and abuse their freedom to choose. As a result, humans are at the same time sinners and saints, subject to history and social forces but also capable of shaping history and society.

Niebuhr used traditional themes found in Scripture (the image of God, the Fall, etc.) to describe humanity's condition, but he always compared them against experience in order to validate their acceptance. In other words, Niebuhr used the biblical view because he agreed with it, not because he felt it was inherently correct.

In the person of Christ, Niebuhr found a unique example of an individual who used power only for good and not (as all other people) for evil. The cross of Christ was a particularly important theme for Niebuhr since it revealed the great paradox of powerlessness turned into power.

The second volume, addressing human destiny, complements the first by proposing a hopeful future for humankind. Niebuhr attempts to summarize the end and meaning of human history.

The Pursuit of God 1948
A. W. Tozer
. . . .

A. W. Tozer was born in Newburg, Pennsylvania, in 1897. At the age of eighteen, Tozer became a Christian. A few years later, without any formal education beyond grade school, he began a lifelong ministry of pastoring several Christian and Missionary Alliance churches in the United States and Canada.

Throughout his Christian life, Tozer was intensely devotional and mystical. He deeply appreciated such mystics as Fénelon, Bernard of Cluny, Bernard of Clairvaux, and Julian of Norwich. Tozer enjoyed devotional poetry, the hymns of the mystics, and the writings of Emerson and Shakespeare. Tozer's spirituality and breadth of reading made his preaching all the more in demand.

Tozer's writings remain as his most lasting impact on the church. Many of his writings were developed from his sermons, including most of his best-known books: *The Pursuit of God* (1948), *The Divine Conquest* (1950), and *The Knowledge of the*

Holy (1961). Tozer's writings focus primarily on knowing God personally and experientially.

In the preface to the first edition of *The Pursuit of God* (1948), A. W. Tozer explains that the purpose of his book is to help readers "taste and know the inner sweetness of the very God Himself in the core and center of their hearts." Tozer was convinced that it is God who nourishes the soul, and "unless and until the hearers find God in personal experience, they are not the better for having heard the truth." In the ten chapters that follow, Tozer tries to introduce his readers to this knowledge of God.

Though Tozer favors "the warm language of personal feeling" throughout the book, he does not hesitate to level harsh indictments against the church regarding its spiritual condition. He decries that "the whole transaction of religious conversion has been made mechanical and spiritless." Tozer calls for a new "heart-theology of fragrant saints" to replace the cold dogma of lifeless theology. But this book is not a polemic; instead, it is Tozer's deliberate attempt to encourage passion for experiencing God.

The Pursuit of God covers several topics as it explores the keys to experiencing God. Throughout the book Tozer includes brief samples from Scripture to support his various points.

Tozer insists that Christians can know God "with at least the same degree of immediacy as they know any other person." Tozer perceives God as universally present in the world. He describes the whole world as being alive with the life of God. Christians have been given the ability to hear the voice of God in the world and the word of God in the Bible. Tozer urges Christians to approach Scripture expecting it to speak to them, rather than treating it like a lifeless object.

Tozer defines faith as the gaze of the heart at God. Such a fixed gaze ushers the Christian into a "spiritual life more in keeping with the promises of God." For Tozer, the disruption of this connection between humans and God is the ultimate cause of misery and suffering. Tozer calls for a restoration of the Creator-creature relationship, where humankind responds to God in the meekness described in Matthew 5.

Tozer closes with a description of life as a sacrament. He cites 1 Corinthians 10:31, "Whether therefore ye eat, or drink, or whatsoever ye do, do all to the glory of God" (KJV).

A. W. Tozer accurately summarized *The Pursuit of God* as presenting nothing new except his own spiritual rediscovery of God. Yet he also added that though his "fire is not large it is yet real, and there may be those who can light their candle at its flame."

Mere Christianity   1952
C. S. Lewis

. . . .

Born in Belfast, Ireland, in 1898, C. S. Lewis grew up in the Anglican Church but became an atheist in his teenage years. He later attended Oxford University, although his studies there were interrupted by military service in World War I. Lewis returned to Oxford and became a fellow of Magdalen College, where he remained for nearly thirty years. During this time Lewis slowly moved from atheism to theism to Christianity. He became a Christian at about age thirty, and shortly afterward he wrote an autobiographical novel called *The Pilgrim's Regress* (1933). His first scholarly work, *The Allegory of Love,* appeared in 1936.

Lewis's newfound faith created a foment of writing during his years at Oxford. For a long time his *Screwtape Letters* (1942) was his most popular work. Lewis wrote this book as a collection of letters from a major devil to a lesser one in charge of a young man's soul. He also wrote *The Problem of Pain* (1940), *Abolition of Man* (1943), *Miracles* (1947), and the Space Trilogy (1938–1945). Another widely read work is *Mere Christianity* (1952), a simple but profound apologetic for Christianity.

In 1954 Lewis accepted the newly created chair of Medieval and Renaissance English at Cambridge University. It was during this same year that his best-known scholarly work, *English Literature in the Sixteenth Century,* was published. Lewis told of his upbringing and conversion in *Surprised by Joy* (1955). Lewis published a series of fiction books called the Chronicles of Narnia (1950–1956), which have become classics for children.

In 1956 Lewis married Joy Davidman Gresham, an American Jewish-Christian who was very ill with cancer. Four years later she died, and Lewis recorded his mourning in *A Grief Observed.*

C. S. Lewis's twenty-five books have sold millions of copies over the years, and several literary societies have been formed in his honor. His combination of sound reasoning, interesting imagery, and understandable language have appealed to countless readers, making his works classic favorites for millions.

Radio talks given by C. S. Lewis in the 1940s are the source for his book *Mere Christianity.* These broadcasts were published as *The Case for Christianity* (1943), *Christian Behaviour* (1943), and *Beyond Personality* (1945) before they were gathered together as *Mere Christianity* in 1952. In his preface Lewis relates his purpose: "I have thought that the best . . . service I could do for my unbelieving neighbours was to explain and defend the belief that has been common to nearly all Christians at all times." It is this that he calls "mere" Christianity.

Book 1 of *Mere Christianity* is titled *Right and Wrong as a Clue to the Meaning of the Universe.* Its five chapters cover the problems of right and wrong behavior, moral law versus instinct, the power that gives force to the law, and the absolute goodness behind moral law. It is at this point that, as Lewis says, "Christianity begins to talk."

Book 2 is titled *What Christians Believe.* Here Lewis first addresses atheism, pantheism, and the Christian idea of God. He then discusses the rebellion of Satan, calling Christianity "the story of how the rightful king has landed" on enemy territory. Concerning Jesus Christ, Lewis challenges the reader to consider: "A man who was merely a man and said the sort of things Jesus said would not be a great moral teacher. He would either be a lunatic . . . or else he would be the Devil of Hell. You must make your choice." Lewis also discusses the atonement and Christ's nature as both divine and human.

Christian Behaviour is the topic of book 3. He analyzes the three parts of morality: harmony between individuals, harmony within the individual, and the general purpose of human life. One chapter is devoted to the cardinal or "pivotal" virtues: prudence, temperance, justice, and fortitude. Another covers the New Testament's description of a fully Christian society. Other chapters address psychoanalysis, sexuality, and marriage. Book 3 closes with discussions about forgiveness, loving your neighbor, pride, and the three "theological virtues" of charity, hope, and faith.

The fourth and final book, *Beyond Personality: or First Steps in the Doctrine of the Trinity*, contains eleven short chapters. Here Lewis discusses theology and refers to it as a "map" of Christianity. Lewis's theological map charts several things: natural human life, spiritual life, the Trinity, time and eternity, the Incarnation, and the meaning of several New Testament phrases, such as "born again" and "be ye perfect."

In *Mere Christianity* C. S. Lewis explains the Christian faith without making direct reference to a single verse of the New Testament. This helps to make the book very understandable for new Christians and unbelievers, who may not be familiar with the Bible. Lewis closes by encouraging the reader to "look for Christ and you will find Him, and with Him everything else thrown in."

The Normal Christian Life 1957
Watchman Nee

. . . .

Watchman Nee (whose real name was Nee Tao Shu) was born in Swatow, China, in 1903. His family then moved to Foochow, where he spent the early part of his life. Nee became a Christian when he was eighteen and gave up the opportunity of attending university, choosing instead to devote himself to Bible study and gospel preaching. He produced a magazine, *The Christian,* which soon had a wide influence. When he was twenty-five, he wrote and published *The Spiritual Man,* a three-volume work explaining the full process of spiritual maturity. Later he started missionary work in Shanghai and had close connections with the China Inland Mission.

Nee was instrumental in establishing churches in many parts of China. These local churches often started as small house churches and were completely independent of foreign missionary organizations. Nee was often criticized for his insistence that there could be only one true local church in each city.

After Pearl Harbor, while living under the Japanese, Nee organized a pharmaceutical company to raise money for the work of the ministry. Nee's intentions in this business venture came to be misunderstood by his fellow workers, however, and consequently Nee had to withdraw from active ministry for several years. This incident would later provide an excuse for his arrest by the Communists.

Following the end of World War II, Watchman Nee was restored to leadership, and the work in Shanghai prospered with large numbers of churches springing up in many parts of the country. Many of these house churches have continued to survive under the Communist government. Watchman Nee was arrested in 1952 while on a trip to Manchuria. Four years later he was brought to Shanghai for a public trial and found guilty of a large number of charges. After serving his fifteen-year sentence, he remained in prison until his death in 1972.

Watchman Nee will be remembered not only for his leadership of an indigenous church movement in China but also for the books that continue to enrich Christians throughout the world. Some of the more noteworthy works are *The Normal Christian Life; Changed into His Likeness; Love Not the World; A Living Sacrifice; Spiritual Man; Sit, Walk, Stand;* and *What Shall This Man Do?*

Watchman Nee's *The Normal Christian Life* bears some likeness to a systematic discourse on Christian doctrine. It was compiled from a series of spoken addresses given in 1938–1939. Nee's initial paragraphs propose that the only one to ever live a normal Christian life is "the Son of God himself." For everyone else, the normal Christian life is summarized by Paul: "I myself no longer live, but Christ lives in me" (Galatians 2:20). The rest of the book explains this concept by referring to Paul's letter to the Romans.

Nee divides Romans into two sections: chapters 1:1–5:11, which discuss how Christ's blood has dealt with what humankind has done, and chapters 5:12–8:39, which show how the Cross deals with what humankind is. "We need the Blood for forgiveness," says Nee. "We need also the Cross for deliverance."

Nee warns against oversimplifying the work of God in a Christian. He urges believers to appreciate the value of Christ's sacrifice and to continually confess known sins to God. He encourages readers to contemplate how they have been freed from the penalty of sin by Jesus Christ's death and resurrection.

These are simply the first steps in Watchman Nee's analysis of the Christian life. The majority of his book covers many other phases of the Christian experience, such as the new birth, deliverance from sin, the gift of the Holy Spirit, and pleasing God. Nee is careful to point out, however, that every Christian's experience is not identical; there is no "rigid pattern" for each Christian, but most believers generally follow this process.

In the final chapter of *The Normal Christian Life,* Watchman Nee considers the gospel story about a woman who anoints Jesus' feet while he is in Simon the Leper's house. This event, to Nee, illustrates the goal of the gospel—that believers would be "wasted for the Lord" so that "the house [can be] filled with the odor of the ointment." Nee concludes: "The Lord grant us grace that we may learn how to please him."

Peace with God   1953
Billy Graham
. . . .

William "Billy" Graham was born November 7, 1918, in Charlotte, North Carolina. His parents owned a dairy farm and were active members of the Associate Presbyterian Church. At the age of sixteen, he became a Christian through the ministry of a Southern evangelist.

After a brief period at Bob Jones College (Tennessee), Graham enrolled in Florida Bible Institute in Tampa, Florida. It was here that Graham made his decision to enter full-time Christian ministry. During this time he began preaching and was ordained as a Southern Baptist minister in 1940. Later that year he enrolled at Wheaton College (Illinois), where he met his future wife, Ruth Bell, the daughter of Presbyterian medical missionaries to China. Billy and Ruth married on August 13, 1943, and they would eventually have five children.

Upon graduation in 1943 with a B.A. in anthropology, Graham became the pastor of a small Baptist church in Western Springs, Illinois. Two years later he resigned to become a full-time evangelist with the newly formed Youth for Christ organization. Almost immediately he began to travel extensively throughout the United States and Great Britain. In 1947 he reluctantly accepted the presidency of the Northwestern Schools in Minneapolis (which included a Bible college, liberal arts college, and seminary) but continued to travel widely as an evangelist, finally resigning from the presidency in 1951.

Graham skyrocketed to national prominence in 1949 through his meetings in Los Angeles. These meetings, which took place in a huge "canvas cathedral" (tent), resulted in the conversion of several well-known personalities and attracted the attention of the media. Almost overnight "Billy Graham" became a household name. In the next few years his citywide evangelistic meetings in stadiums and arenas established a pattern for mass evangelism that would always be associated with his ministry. He has preached in person in more than eighty countries to over 110 million people, more than any other individual in history. Hundreds of millions more have heard him through television, radio, and film.

Graham's primary commitment has always been to preach the message of the Christian faith to nonbelievers. This desire led him to utilize the mass media for spreading this message to an unprecedented extent. His worldwide radio program, *The Hour of Decision,* started in 1950, soon was heard on hundreds of stations. He used television extensively almost as soon as it became a widespread medium. Several times a year Graham's organization purchased prime time for several days on major stations, rather than attempting a weekly production. As technology has advanced, Graham has used satellites and videotapes to extend single crusade meetings across entire continents.

Graham has authored over fifteen books, most of which have hit the best-seller lists and have been widely translated. He also is a frequent guest on major television programs.

While drawing upon the work of earlier evangelists, such as John Wesley, George Whitefield, and Charles Finney, Graham sought to refine and update the methods of mass evangelism.

Each citywide "crusade" was carefully organized, using trained staff to work with local church leaders and volunteers for many months in advance. Early in his work Graham realized the need for more effective follow-up of those making spiritual commitments in his meetings. He developed a system that includes basic Bible studies, personal counseling, and immediate contact with a local church.

Almost from the beginning of his public ministry, Graham opted for a cooperative approach to evangelism, working with all churches and denominations that would cooperate with him. This led to criticism from both fundamentalists and liberals. Fundamentalists denounced him for "compromising" with liberal churches and clergymen, and liberals rejected his message and methods as simplistic, out-of-date, and socially irrelevant. Many conservative critics also assailed him for integrating his meetings, which he did more than a year before the Supreme Court's landmark decision on civil rights (1954). In the late 1970s and early 1980s, others criticized him for accepting invitations to preach in Communist-dominated Eastern Europe and the Soviet Union.

In spite of these critics, however, Graham's integrity, personal humility, and popular appeal have made him one of the most influential religious leaders of the twentieth century. The annual Gallup Poll has repeatedly ranked him among the ten most admired men in America since 1951. He has sometimes been called the unofficial White House chaplain, due to his friendship with every American president since Harry Truman. He has received numerous honorary degrees and over fifty major awards, including the Templeton Prize for Progress in Religion (1982) and the Presidential Medal of Freedom (1983), America's highest nonmilitary honor.

Of special significance is Graham's influence on the resurgence of evangelical Christianity in the latter half of the twentieth century. As the most visible proponent of biblical Christianity, Graham has become the symbolic leader of evangelicalism, in spite of his refusal to become associated with special interest groups or causes. His concern for the future of evangelicalism led him to found Christianity Today, Inc., which publishes several evangelical magazines. He continues to serve as chairman of the board. Graham has also used his influence to draw together evangelical leaders in a series of international congresses to discuss plans for world evangelism. He has also served on the boards of Gordon-Conwell Theological Seminary (Massachusetts) and of Wheaton College (Illinois).

Billy Graham opens his book *Peace with God* by asserting: "I am convinced that there is a great hunger of mind and thirst of soul on the part of the average man for peace with God." Published in 1953, this book provides basic spiritual information in simple form so that the uninitiated reader might understand the basic message of Christianity and be built up in the faith.

The book is divided into three parts, each with six chapters. Part 1, "The Problem," begins with a chapter entitled "The Quest." Here Graham describes humanity's search for solutions to the problems that have come from the Fall (Genesis 1). These three problems are sin, sorrow, and death.

Chapter 2 examines why the Bible "has endured and been man's unfailing source of faith and spiritual strength." In chapter 3 Graham answers such questions as: Who is God? What is he like? How can we be sure he exists? When did he begin? Can we know him? Chapter 4 covers the problem of sin, and chapter 5 contemplates the devil, who is to blame for the suffering in the world. "After Death—What?" completes part 1. Here Graham affirms the reality of death, hell, and heaven.

Part 2, "The Solution," begins with chapter 7, "Why Jesus Came." This chapter explains God's purpose in the Incarnation, death, and resurrection of Jesus Christ. Chapter 8 explains "How and Where to Begin" in becoming a Christian. Graham asserts that conversion involves three steps—repentance, faith, and regeneration. The next three chapters deal with these three steps. Part 2 concludes with "How to Be Sure."

"The Results" of God's salvation is the topic of part 3. "The Enemies of the Christian," chapter 13, covers the devil, the world system, and worldly lust, and how to overcome them. "Rules of the Christian Life" are outlined in chapter 14. Chapter 15 addresses "The Christian and the Church." Graham covers the "Social Obligations of the Christian" in chapter 16. The next chapter, "The Future of the Christian," discusses the return of Christ. The final chapter of this simple yet significant book is "Peace—at Last." Here Billy Graham lists the many benefits of becoming a Christian. In closing, Graham assures believers, "The storm rages, but our hearts are at rest. We have found peace—at last!"

TIMELINE

c. 30	Jesus' crucifixion and resurrection
70	The destruction of the temple in Jerusalem
132	Bar Kokhba leads a revolt in Palestine
324	Constantine secures his rule over the Roman Empire
395	The Roman Empire is divided into East and West
410	Barbarians attack Rome
c. 570	Muhammad is born
800	Charlemagne is crowned emperor of the Holy Roman Empire
1054	The Church officially splits, separating Roman Catholicism from Eastern Orthodoxy
1066	William of Normandy conquers England
1095	The first Crusade
1215	The Magna Carta is drafted
c. 1348	Black Death spreads throughout Europe
c. 1450	Johannes Gutenberg invents his printing press
1492	Christopher Columbus arrives in the New World
1504	Michelangelo completes his sculpture of David
1517	Martin Luther nails his Ninety-five Theses to the chapel door
1534	Henry VIII establishes the Church of England
1536	William Tyndale is strangled and burned at the stake
1543	Nicolaus Copernicus publishes *On the Revolutions of Heavenly Spheres*
1563	Council of Trent is adjourned
1616	William Shakespeare dies
1620	Pilgrims arrive in America
1640	The English Civil War
1769	James Watt invents the steam engine
1776	The American Revolution
1789	The French Revolution
1815	Napoleon Bonaparte is defeated at Waterloo
1848	Karl Marx publishes his *Communist Manifesto*
1859	Charles Darwin publishes *On the Origin of Species by Means of Natural Selection*
1865	The American Civil War ends
1918	World War I ends
1929	The Great Depression begins in America
1945	World War II ends

BIBLIOGRAPHY

Note to the reader: The following is a list of sources where readers may find the complete texts of works summarized in this book. The sources are listed in the order in which they appear in the summaries.

The Early Church Fathers
Lightfoot, J. B., and J. R. Harmer, eds. *The Apostolic Fathers.* Grand Rapids: Baker, 1992.

Irenaeus. *The Scandal of the Incarnation: Irenaeus Against the Heresies.* Translated by John Seward. San Francisco: Ignatius Press, 1990.

Schaff, Philip, and Henry Wace, eds. *Nicene and Post-Nicene Fathers.* Vol. 14, *The Seven Ecumenical Councils.* Early Church Fathers Series, no. 2. Peabody, Mass.: Hendrickson Publishers, 1994.

The Middle Ages
Augustine of Hippo. *Confessions of Saint Augustine.* Translated by Edward B. Pusey. New York: Macmillan, 1961.

————. *City of God.* Translated by Marcus Dods. New York: Random House, 1977.

Benedict of Nursia. *Rule of Saint Benedict.* Translated by Anthony C. Meisel and M. L. Del Mastro. New York: Doubleday and Company, 1975.

Anselm of Canterbury. *St. Anselm.* Translated by Sidney Norton Deane. La Salle, Ill.: The Open Court Publishing Company, 1951.

Bernard of Clairvaux. *Sermons on the Song of Songs.* Cistercian Fathers Series. Kalamazoo, Mich.: Cistercian Publications, no date.

St. Bonaventure. *The Works of Bonaventure.* Vol. 1. Translated by Jose de Vinck. Cincinnati, Ohio: St. Anthony's Guild Press, 1960.

Thomas Aquinas. *Summa Theologica of Saint Thomas Aquinas.* 5 vols. Westminster, Md.: Christian Classics, 1981.

Dante Alighieri. *Divine Comedy.* Translated by Charles H. Sisson. New York: Oxford University Press, 1993.

Julian of Norwich. *Revelations of Divine Love: Juliana of Norwich.* Translated by M. L. Del Mastro. New York: Doubleday, 1977.

Thomas à Kempis. *Imitation of Christ.* Translated by Leo Shirley-Price. New York: Viking Penguin, 1952.

The Renaissance and Reformation
Farstad, Arthur L., and Zane C. Hodges, eds. *The Greek New Testament According to the Majority Text.* Nashville: Nelson, 1982.

Tyndale, William. *Tyndale's New Testament.* New Haven, Conn.: Yale University Press, 1989.

Luther, Martin. *Luther's Works.* Vol. 27, *Lectures on Galatians,* edited by Jaroslav Pelikan. St. Louis: Concordia Publishing House, 1964.

Reu, Johann M., ed. *Augsburg Confession.* New York: AMS Pr., Inc., 1930.

Calvin, John. *Institutes of the Christian Religion.* 1536 ed. Translated by Ford L. Battles. Grand Rapids: Eerdmans, 1986.

Milton, John. *Paradise Lost.* Cutchogue, N.Y.: Buccaneer Books, 1983.

Spener, Philipp Jakob. *Pia Desideria.* Edited and translated by Theodore G. Tappert. Minneapolis: Augsburg Fortress, 1964.

Bunyan, John. *The Pilgrim's Progress.* Grand Rapids: Baker Book House, 1984.

Brother Lawrence. *The Practice of the Presence of God.* Grand Rapids: Baker Book House, 1980.

The Eighteenth and Nineteenth Centuries

Law, William. *A Serious Call to a Devout and Holy Life.* Ridgefield, Conn.: Morehouse Publishing, 1982.

Edwards, Jonathan. *A Treatise Concerning Religious Affections.* Irvine, Calif.: Reprint Services Corporation, 1992.

Woolman, John. *The Journal and Major Essays of John Woolman.* Irvine, Calif.: Reprint Services Corporation, 1991.

Wesley, John. *The Journal of John Wesley: A Selection.* Edited by Elisabeth Jay. New York: Oxford University Press, 1987.

Westcott, B. F., and J. F. Hort. *Introduction to the New Testament in the Original Greek.* Peabody, Mass.: Hendrickson Publishers, 1988.

Murray, Andrew. *Abide in Christ.* Grand Rapids: Zondervan, 1990.

Sheldon, Charles. *In His Steps.* Waco, Tex.: Word, 1988.

The Twentieth Century

Rauschenbusch, Walter. *A Theology for the Social Gospel.* New York: Macmillan, 1917.

Barth, Karl. *Church Dogmatics.* Vols. 1–4. Edited by G. W. Bromiley and T. F. Torrence. Herndon, Va.: Books International, 1956–1969.

Chambers, Oswald. *My Utmost for His Highest.* Grand Rapids: Discovery House Publishers, 1989.

Bonhoeffer, Dietrich. *The Cost of Discipleship.* New York: Macmillan, 1963.

Niebuhr, Reinhold. *The Nature and Destiny of Man.* Vol. 1. New York: Scribners, 1941.

Tozer, A. W. *The Pursuit of God.* Shalimar, Fla.: Christian Publications, 1982.

Lewis, C. S. *Mere Christianity.* New York: Macmillan, 1986.

Watchman Nee. *The Normal Christian Life.* Wheaton, Ill.: Tyndale House Publishers, 1977.

Graham, Billy. *Peace with God.* Waco, Tex.: Word, 1984.